CD INCLUDED

99 DEMO TRACKS

THE GUITARIST'S
SURVIVAL KIT

EVERYTHING YOU NEED TO KNOW TO BE A WORKING MUSICIAN

Guitar parts performed by Doug Boduch

ISBN 0-634-00604-5

HAL•LEONARD®
CORPORATION
7777 W. BLUEMOUND RD. P.O. BOX 13819 MILWAUKEE, WI 53213

Visit Hal Leonard Online at
www.halleonard.com

INTRODUCTION

Consider this: A guitarist is a musician, and being a musician is a trade. The ability to succeed at any trade requires being proficient at several different areas within your chosen field—this is where the phrase "learning the tools of the trade" comes from. For working musicians, some of the most lucrative jobs are wedding gigs, while some of the most common, consistent, and dependable (and, to some, the most fun) are bar band gigs. If you plan on making a living as a musician, and you're not a player of the "rock star" or "session ace" variety, these are the kinds of jobs that will put bread on the table. But if you want these "jobs," some behind-the-scenes preparation needs to take place. Regardless of the musical endeavor, if you blow it, you most likely won't get called back by the event's contractor or music director, let alone get referred to another gig by a respected player—until you get your act together.

The bottom line? You need to be ready for anything when it comes time to play. Your bandleader may call off a tune you don't know. If this happens, you'd better be able to "fake" your way through it, regardless of the style. What if he or she points to you midway through a tune, expecting you to whip off an impromptu guitar solo—in a song or style you've never played before? What would you do? Relax. You can survive any of these scenarios if you have a back-up bag of basics to bail yourself out. Enter *The Guitarist's Survival Kit*.

This book is broken down into five sections: songs and set lists, gear, rhythm riffs, lead licks, and transposition. Becoming thoroughly familiar with the material in each of these categories will give you confidence in knowing that you can "get by" and survive any musical situation—even the occasional nightmare gig.

Incidentally, the contents of this book are being presented under the assumption that the reader already has a "professional attitude" and exudes "professionalism" in the first place. This means that you have a pleasant demeanor, professional attire (ranging from jeans and a T-shirt to a tuxedo), and access to reliable transportation (i.e., you are never late). Further, it's assumed that you always exercise common sense, musically speaking. This means your new strings are "in tune" before you get on stage. And, perhaps most importantly, you never "overplay"— demonstrating a lack of musical taste is one of the quickest ways to get yourself booted (or, at the very least, booed) off the bandstand. Lastly, it's presumed that you possess a "better safe than sorry" mentality. This means that you always have the following: extra tubes and fuses on hand in the event that your amp blows one, multiple sets of electric and acoustic (nylon and steel) guitar strings on hand, and a host of functional cords that run virtually no risk of shorting out—this would include several guitar cords of varying lengths in case someone decides you need to move farther away from your amp, as well as an extension cord in the event that the band is positioned far from an available outlet. Think about it: If you can't quickly resolve the inevitable gear-related problems unique to playing guitar, imagine the opinion your fellow musician will have of you. Having the foresight to cover all these bases will provide you with a mental "safety net," and this will enable you to play more confidently, freeing your mind to focus on the music.

With that said, let's get to it...

ABOUT THE AUTHOR

Dale Turner has authored numerous guitar instructional books for Hal Leonard Corporation and Cherry Lane Music, and transcribed dozens of note-for-note album folios for most of the nation's major publishers. He is currently the West Coast Editor of *GuitarOne* magazine, where he contributes everything from interview features and instructional pieces to performance notes and song transcriptions. Dale's written work has also appeared in *Guitar World, Guitar (For the Practicing Musician), Guitar School, Maximum Guitar, Guitar Techniques* (a UK publication), and *Guitar Player* magazines. A member of David Pritchard's Acoustic Guitar Quartet, Dale has performed with an array of renowned players—including Billy Cobham (Mahavishnu Orchestra/Miles Davis), Larry Klein (Joni Mitchell/Shawn Colvin), Eric "Bobo" Correa (Cypress Hill), and Josh Levy (Big Bad Voodoo Daddy), among others. He uses D'Addario strings and picks, exclusively. In 1991, Mr. Turner received his bachelor's degree in Studio Guitar Performance from the University of Southern California where he subsequently taught as a part-time pop/rock guitar instructor/lecturer (1993-95).

SONGS & SET LISTS

MUST-KNOW TUNES FOR EVERY OCCASION

One of the most basic requirements of being a working musician is having a solid repertoire. This means being proficient in a variety of styles and tunes so that you have something appropriate to play during the event for which you've been hired. Regardless of whether you're playing at a wedding or for a bunch of blasted boozers at a bar, every conceivable gig actually has a clear-cut set of songs—or "standards"—that are time-tested and fail-safe. The audience probably knows most of them because they've been on the radio for years, and, like it or not, they're things you're *expected* to play by whomever is paying you.

Depending upon the situation, these songs can run the stylistic gamut. If you're playing a wedding, be prepared to cover everything from blues, reggae and funk, to jazz, country, and rock—even polka! On the other hand, if you're about to play a bar gig, be ready to toss in one of the current radio hits—usually something new that's high on the Billboard "Modern Rock" chart. In instances where you've been contracted to play an evening of music within a specific genre (e.g., "jazz," "blues," or "country"), you'd better make sure you have—at minimum—*ten* tunes synonymous with that musical style memorized or charted out in advance. As another incentive, remember this: a band with an extensive repertoire is capable of taking a wide range of song requests—your ability to perform a tune requested by the bride's mother will impress the folks who sign your check!

All totaled, the combined length of all the selections you choose to play at a given event will most likely need to fit within a 45-minute time frame, or "set." (This constitutes an hour because you're entitled to take a fifteen-minute break.) By having ten of the "right" tunes under your belt (ten four- or five-minute songs equal approx. 45 minutes), you just might "survive" one of these types of gigs. Keeping in mind that most bands get hired to play for at least three hours, you'll need to have multiple sets worth of material up and running! Below is a list of songs (and the artists who made them famous) that are mandatory when it comes to playing the most basic of gigs: performing at a wedding reception, or as a "bar band." Think of each list as your first 45-minute set:

TEN MUST-KNOW WEDDING SONGS

1) "Beer Barrel Polka"—Bobby Vinton
2) "Could I Have This Dance"—Anne Murray
3) "Dance Little Bird (The Chicken Dance)"—Standard
4) "I Knew the Bride (When She Used to Rock 'n' Roll)"—Nick Lowe
5) "Mony Mony"—Tommy James and the Shondells/Billy Idol
6) "Old Time Rock & Roll"—Bob Seger
7) "Proud Mary"—Creedence Clearwater Revival/Ike and Tina Turner
8) "Tequila"—The Champs
9) "Twist and Shout"—The Isley Brothers/The Beatles
10) "Wipe Out"—The Surfaris

TEN MUST-KNOW BAR-BAND SONGS

1) "Brown Eyed Girl"—Van Morrison
2) "It's Still Rock and Roll to Me"—Billy Joel
3) "Margaritaville"—Jimmy Buffett
4) "Mustang Sally"—Eric Clapton/Commitments
5) "Only Wanna Be With You"—Hootie and the Blowfish
6) "Pretty Woman"—Roy Orbison/Van Halen
7) "Sweet Home Alabama"—Lynyrd Skynyrd
8) "Takin' Care of Business"—Bachman Turner Overdrive
9) "Smooth"—Santana
10) "Wonderful Tonight"—Eric Clapton

Note the diversity in artists represented in each of these lists. With the exception of the goofier songs like "Beer Barrel Polka" and "Chicken Dance," and tunes that have audience participation built in (*á la* the "Hokey Pokey," "Electric Slide," and "Macarena"), almost all the songs on both lists fall into the "classic rock" category. This means most people will relate to them. Another common denominator among both sets is the high percentage of danceable tunes. Remember: The people you're playing for want to be on the dance floor having a good time, plus the owner of the bar wants to keep them dancing so they get thirsty. At the same time, keep in mind that the tempos and subject matter of the songs should vary over the course of a set. Be sure to mix in slow dance songs, fun songs, and songs that flat-out rock.

Many of these songs also have signature guitar parts, and if you don't play them exactly right, the audience or dancers may not recognize them. Do yourself a favor and get a few of these babies under your belt (you may need to purchase a few songbooks or do some transcribing), realizing that once you learn them—provided you work fairly regularly—you'll never forget them. These guitar-based songs are also invaluable when you find yourself confronted with a "spontaneous jam" situation, or when you are asked to "sit in" with your buddy's band.

What follows is a collection of possible set lists for various "genre-specific" gigs. Selections from these lists can also be used to augment a set of "bar band" or "wedding band" material:

TEN MUST-KNOW BALLADS

1) "Candle in the Wind"—Elton John
2) "Crazy"—Patsy Cline
3) "Desperado"—The Eagles
4) "Every Breath You Take"—The Police
5) "Let It Be"—The Beatles
6) "Love Me Tender"—Elvis Presley
7) "Tears in Heaven"—Eric Clapton
8) "When a Man Loves a Woman"—Percy Sledge/Michael Bolton
9) "Yesterday"—The Beatles
10) "You Are So Beautiful"—Joe Cocker

TEN MUST-KNOW CHRISTMAS SONGS

1) "The Christmas Song (Chestnuts Roasting on an Open Fire)"
2) "Deck the Halls"
3) "Feliz Navidad"
4) "Have Yourself a Merry Little Christmas"
5) "Rudolph the Red-Nosed Reindeer"
6) "Santa Claus is Comin' to Town"
7) "Silent Night"
8) "Silver Bells"
9) "We Wish You a Merry Christmas"
10) "White Christmas"

TEN MUST-KNOW CLASSIC ROCK SONGS

1) "Day Tripper"—The Beatles
2) "Freebird"—Lynyrd Skynyrd
3) "Little Wing"—Jimi Hendrix
4) "More Than a Feeling"—Boston
5) "Roadhouse Blues"—The Doors
6) "Satisfaction"—Rolling Stones
7) "Take It Easy"—The Eagles/Jackson Browne
8) "Walk This Way"—Aerosmith
9) "You Really Got Me"—The Kinks/Van Halen
10) "You Shook Me All Night Long"—AC/DC

TEN MUST-KNOW BLUES SONGS

1) "Born Under a Bad Sign"—Albert King/Eric Clapton/Robben Ford
2) "Crossroads"—Robert Johnson/Cream
3) "Hideaway"—Freddie King/Eric Clapton w/Bluesbreakers
4) "Hoochie Coochie Man"—Muddy Waters/Eric Clapton/Jimi Hendrix
5) "I Just Wanna Make Love to You"—Muddy Waters/Rolling Stones
6) "I'm a Man"—Bo Diddley
7) "Pride and Joy"—Stevie Ray Vaughan
8) "Red House"—Jimi Hendrix
9) "Stormy Monday Blues"—T-Bone Walker/Allman Brothers Band
10) "The Thrill Is Gone"—B.B. King

TEN MUST-KNOW COUNTRY SONGS

1) "Blue Eyes Crying in the Rain"—Fred Rose/Willie Nelson
2) "The Devil Went Down to Georgia"—Charlie Daniels Band
3) "The Gambler"—Kenny Rogers
4) "Hey Good Lookin' "—Hank Williams
5) "I Walk the Line"—Johnny Cash
6) "Mamas Don't Let Your Babies Grow Up to Be Cowboys"—Waylon Jennings
7) "On the Road Again"—Willie Nelson
8) "Stand By Your Man"—Loretta Lynn
9) "Take Me Home, Country Roads"—John Denver
10) "That's Alright Mama"—A. Crudup, J. Johnson/Elvis Presley

TEN MUST-KNOW FRATERNITY-PARTY FAVORITES

1) "Bad to the Bone"—George Thorogood and the Destroyers
2) "Born to Be Wild"—Steppenwolf
3) "(You Gotta) Fight For Your Right (To Party!)"—Beastie Boys
4) "Let's Get Stoned"—Ray Charles/Joe Cocker
5) "Louie Louie"—The Kingsmen
6) "My Ding-A-Ling"—Chuck Berry
7) "Why Don't We Get Drunk (and Screw)?"—Jimmy Buffett
8) "Should I Stay or Should I Go?"—The Clash
9) "Shout"—The Isley Brothers
10) "The Joker"—Steve Miller Band

TEN INVALUABLE INSTRUMENTAL CLASSICS

1) "Chameleon"—Herbie Hancock
2) "Europa (Earth's Cry, Heaven's Smile)"—Carlos Santana
3) "Freeway Jam"—Jeff Beck
4) "Jean-Pierre"—Miles Davis
5) "Jessica"—The Allman Brothers Band
6) "Misirlou"—Dick Dale and the Del-Tones
7) "Peter Gunn Theme"—Henry Mancini/Duane Eddy
8) "Pipeline"—The Chantays
9) "Sleepwalk"—Santo & Johnny Farina/Larry Carlton
10) "Watermelon Man"—Herbie Hancock

TEN MUST-KNOW JAZZ STANDARDS

1) "All the Things You Are"—Oscar Hammerstein and Jerome Kern
2) "Autumn Leaves"—Joseph Kosma and Johnny Mercer
3) "Billie's Bounce"—Charlie Parker
4) "Blue Bossa"—Kenny Dorham
5) "Days of Wine and Roses"—Henry Mancini
6) "I Got Rhythm"/"Oleo"—George Gershwin/Sonny Rollins
7) "So What?"/"Impressions"—Miles Davis/John Coltrane
8) "My Romance"—Rodgers and Hart
9) "Someday My Prince Will Come"—Morey and Churchill
10) "Stella by Starlight"—Victor Young

TEN MUST-KNOW MOTOWN/'60S R&B SONGS

1) "(Sittin' On) The Dock of the Bay"—
   Otis Redding and Steve Cropper
2) "Hard to Handle"—Otis Redding/Grateful Dead/Black Crowes
3) "I Heard It Through the Grapevine"—Marvin Gaye
4) "Knock On Wood"—Eddie Floyd and Steve Cropper/Amii Stewart
5) "Let's Get It On"—Marvin Gaye
6) "My Girl"—The Temptations
7) "Soul Man"—Sam & Dave/Blues Brothers
8) "Stand By Me"—Ben E. King
9) "Try a Little Tenderness"—Otis Redding/Al Jarreau
10) "What's Goin' On?"—Marvin Gaye

TEN MUST-KNOW FUNKY/GROOVY TUNES

1) "Brick House"—The Commodores
2) "Flash Light"—Parliament
3) "Funk #49"—The James Gang
4) "Get Up (I Feel Like Being a Sex Machine)"—James Brown
5) "Le Freak"—Chic
6) "Love Rollercoaster"—The Ohio Players/Red Hot Chili Peppers
7) "Papa's Got a Brand New Bag"—James Brown
8) "Play That Funky Music (White Boy)"—Wild Cherry
9) "Shining Star"—Earth, Wind & Fire
10) "Superstition"—Stevie Wonder/Stevie Ray Vaughan

TEN MUST-KNOW REGGAE SONGS

1) "Baby, I Love Your Way"—covered by Big Mountain
2) "Could You Be Loved"—Bob Marley and the Wailers
3) "Get Up Stand Up"—Bob Marley and the Wailers
4) "I Shot the Sheriff"—Bob Marley and the Wailers/Eric Clapton
5) "Jamming"—Bob Marley and the Wailers
6) "Lively Up Yourself"—Bob Marley and the Wailers
7) "Red Red Wine"—covered by UB40
8) "So Much Trouble in the World"—Bob Marley and the Wailers
9) "Stepping Razor"—Peter Tosh
10) "Tomorrow People"—Ziggy Marley

TEN MUST-KNOW TUNES FOR MISCELLANEOUS CELEBRATIONS/EVENTS

1) "Amazing Grace" (Funeral)
2) "Auld Lang Syne" (New Year's Eve)
3) "Coronation March" (Graduation)
4) "The Dreidel Song" (Hanukkah)
5) "Happy Birthday" (Birthday)
6) "Jesu, Joy of Man's Desiring" (Wedding/Christmas)
7) "Monster Mash" (Halloween)—Bobby "Boris" Pickett
8) "Stars and Stripes Forever" (Fourth of July)
9) "Star-Spangled Banner"
   (Sporting Events/Events of National Interest)
10) "When Irish Eyes Are Smiling" (St. Patrick's Day)

GUITARS, AMPS, EFFECTS, AND HOW TO USE THEM

From one musical style to another, the guitar's tone can change dramatically. This is a direct result of specific gear combinations—different guitars, amplifiers, and effects—being employed in unique ways within each genre. Since most of us don't have the luxury of owning a million different sounding guitars—like a Stratocaster, Telecaster, Les Paul, Rickenbacker electric 12-string, ES-335, and ES-175—we usually have to make do with what we have. Most of the aforementioned guitars can "cut the mustard"—or sound stylistically in the ballpark—with a little ingenuity, but each instrument has its own area of specialty. For instance, a Les Paul will sound great in a rock, blues, and even modern jazz context, but it would probably be the last instrument you'd plug in when playing a country gig. Similarly, an ES-335 will be perfect for a blues or modern jazz gig, but would likely get you booted out of an '80s metal cover band. Telecasters are very versatile when it comes to playing country, blues, rock, and even jazz, but can't quite cop the characteristic clunk of funk. Your Rickenbacker electric 12-string certainly will bring a Beatles tune to life, but it would sound ridiculous if you were playing "chord melody"-style on a solo jazz guitar gig. Meanwhile, a large, hollowbody electric—like a Gibson ES-175 or Super 400—will be perfect for any jazz gig but is impractical for virtually any other style. Finally, a Stratocaster is arguably the most versatile of all the above, equally adaptable to rock, blues, funk, country, and reggae styles. Add to this list the variety of acoustic instruments and their appropriate stylistic surroundings, and—to the inexperienced—the quantity of gear you might think you'd need for a single gig could seem endless.

What follows is a general overview of the types of guitars, amps, and effects typically found within each basic genre, and a list of the players who used them. In most cases, certain tone tips are included. These tonal "shortcuts" are intended to help players closely approximate the characteristic tone of each style when you need to "make do" with a garden-variety setup.

BLUES

TONE CHARACTERISTICS: Most blues guitarists opt for a stinging Strat tone or the warmer sound of a semi-hollowbody electric, played through a slightly-to-moderately overdriven tube amp. Strat-style guitars are often equipped with heavy gauge strings (for a meatier tone), played using either neck, or middle and neck pickups.

GUITARS: Strat-style (Buddy Guy, Eric Clapton, Stevie Ray Vaughan, Robert Cray), Gibson Les Paul (Mike Bloomfield, Eric Clapton w/Bluesbreakers and Cream), Gibson ES-335 (Larry Carlton), ES-345, or ES-355 (B.B. King, Freddie King, John Lee Hooker, Hubert Sumlin).

AMPS: Fender Tweed Bassman, Super Reverb, Twin Reverb, Vibrasonic, Tone Master, Marshall Bluesbreaker Combo, Matchless, and Dumble.

STRINGS: Heavier strings (from .10 to .014) are often used, particularly among performers who tune their instrument down 1/2 step (e.g., Stevie Ray Vaughan).

EFFECTS: Players like Stevie Ray Vaughan use an Ibanez Tube Screamer (TS-808 or TS-9) for extra distortion, using the unit to push their leads over the top. The wah-wah pedal is also commonly employed.

TONE TIPS: Fire up your amp's gain section, and back off on your guitar's volume till you arrive at a tone that just barely breaks up, yet is saturated enough to offer adequate sustain. A tube amp will give you sufficient headroom to vary your dynamics simply by making adjustments in your pick attack.

COUNTRY

TONE CHARACTERISTICS: Typically, electrified country is played on either a Tele (bridge pickup) or a Strat (back two pickups), using a twangy clean tone through vintage Fender amps.

ELECTRIC GUITARS: Fender Telecaster (Albert Lee, Roy Buchanan, James Burton, Steve Cropper, the Hellecasters' guitarists) or Stratocaster (Vince Gill).

ACOUSTIC GUITARS: Martin acoustic guitars are standard, though electrified Ovation acoustics are a favorite among some players when performing live.

AMPS: Fender Twin or Fender Bassman.

STRINGS AND ACCESSORIES: Electrics are often strung with light-gauge strings (.08) to facilitate bending, and equipped with a "hard-tail" bridge (i.e., nontremolo "fixed" bridge) to maintain intonation when executing double-stop bends or bends used in conjunction with stationary notes. Some guitars are also fitted with a Parsons B-Bender. This device is attached to the bridge and, when manipulated by pulling on the guitar's strap, raises the pitch of the B string, creating a pedal-steel effect. Meanwhile, acoustic guitar parts are typically played in open position for the characteristic "jangle"—a sound only attainable by using open strings—with a capo used to change keys.

FUNK

TONE CHARACTERISTICS: Semi-clean, snapping Strat tone, often inflected with various psychedelic sounds from an assortment of pedal effects. Also, clunky-sounding single-note riffs, courtesy of a specific right/left-hand attack.

GUITARS: Strat-style guitars are preferable because their unique pickup configuration (with five-way switch) can produce well-rounded yet percussive tones. A Strat's tone can also easily cut through a typical funk band's added instrumentation (e.g., horns and occasional synths). However, because the guitar's role is primarily percussive, most solidbody electric guitars work fine if EQ'd properly.

EFFECTS: Some of the more psychedelic effects used include the wah-wah pedal (*á la* Jimi Hendrix's intro to "Voodoo Child" or the characteristic "chucka-chucka" funky scratches unique to the opening and closing of a wah-wah pedal while muted strings are struck), phase shifter, and envelope filter.

TONE TIPS: Funk is most effective when played through an amp with just a touch of gain, backing off slightly on the guitar's volume from its volume knob (so you can really dig in). Also, most funk players use a Strat-style guitar in either of its "out-of-phase" positions (bridge-and-middle or neck-and-middle pickups). A key ingredient in achieving a characteristic funk tone is the percussive attack that's created by aggressively smacking a handful of muted strings, while letting only the intended notes ring out.

CLASSIC ROCK

TONE CHARACTERISTICS: Wide array of tones created with an assortment of vintage gear.

TYPICAL INSTRUMENT/AMP COMBINATIONS: *Beatles:* Fender Telecaster, Gretsch, and Rickenbacker (12-string electric) guitars through Vox amps (AC-30). *Rolling Stones:* Fender Telecaster into Ampeg or Fender amps. *Cream:* Gibson Les Paul or SG through Marshall. (Note: Clapton frequently used his guitar's neck pickup with the tone control set near "0" when he took a solo.) *Jimi Hendrix:* Stratocaster (equipped w/tremolo bar) through Marshall 100-watt stacks (Super Bass heads and Super Lead heads) and Fuzz Face distortion unit for "over-the-top" stuff. Also, wah-wah and octaver for some leads.

METAL/HARD ROCK

A) '70S METAL (OR "CLASSIC METAL")/HARD ROCK

TONE CHARACTERISTICS: Metallic, bass-heavy fuzz tone.

FAVORED INSTRUMENT/AMP COMBINATIONS: *Black Sabbath:* Gibson SG through a 100-watt Laney head. For extra gain, Iommi used a customized Rangemaster to boost his amp's volume and treble frequencies. *Led Zeppelin:* Gibson Les Paul Standard or Fender Telecaster through Vox AC-30, Fender Supro Amp (when recording), or 100-watt Marshall (when playing live). *AC/DC:* Angus Young uses a Gibson SG through Marshall JTM 45; Malcolm Young uses a 1963 Gretsch Jet Firebird.

B) '80S METAL/HARD ROCK

TONE CHARACTERISTICS: Crunchy distortion achieved via a scooped-out midrange, with boosted high and low frequencies.

TYPICAL INSTRUMENT/AMP COMBINATIONS: *Van Halen, Ratt,* and *Dokken:* Strat-style solidbody electric (e.g., Kramer, Charvel/Jackson, ESP) with single humbucker pickup in bridge position, single volume control, and Floyd Rose tremolo system. B.C. Rich, Ibanez, Hamer, and Steinberger guitars also used by various artists. Guitars typically played through Marshall, Randall, and Laney stacks, or MESA/Boogie. Rockman amp occasionally used for direct recording (Boston, Dokken). Soldano amps used by many rock session players (Steve Lukather, Mike Landau).

EFFECTS: MXR Phase 90, flanger, and Univox EC-80 echo unit (Edward Van Halen). Wah-wah pedal for melodic parts (Steve Vai, Joe Satriani) or used as tone filter (Michael Schenker, Matthias Jabs). Chorus effect on clean and some distorted rhythm guitar parts. Digital delay for chimey clean parts, echo-repeat riffs, echo trails at end of lead phrases.

C) EARLY-'90S GRUNGE AND LATE-'90S METAL

TONE CHARACTERISTICS: Grunge is characterized as a stripped-down sound, courtesy of combining cheap guitars with sickly distorted amps. A derivative of Drop D tuning is also frequently employed. Late-'90s Metal uses a combination of experimental effects with ultra heavy tones, the heaviness due in part to the genre's drastically detuned guitars.

TYPICAL INSTRUMENT/AMP COMBINATIONS: *Nirvana:* Fender Mustangs and Jaguars through Mesa/Boogie preamp, Crown power amp, and Roland EF-1 distortion box. *Soundgarden:* Solidbody electric (Guild S-100/Gretsch Tennesseean) equipped with humbucking pickups, played through Mesa/Boogie Dual Rectifiers. *Alice In Chains:* G&L Rampage Strat through Bogner Fish, Mesa/Boogie Dual Rectifier, or Peavey 5150. *Metallica:* ESP guitars through Mesa/Boogie Mark II-C heads through Marshall cabinet. *Korn:* Detuned Ibanez 7-string guitars played through Rivera, Mesa/Boogie, Bogner, or Hughes and Kettner amps.

EFFECTS: Digitech Whammy Pedal (Rage Against the Machine, Korn, Pantera), Big Muff distortion pedal (Smashing Pumpkins, Korn), wah-wah (Alice In Chains), envelope filter (Korn, Limp Bizkit), E-Bow, and miscellaneous tremolo effects.

JAZZ

TONE CHARACTERISTICS: Warm, clean tone with boosted midrange.

GUITARS: Gibson L-5, Super 400 (Tuck Andress), ES-175 (Wes Montgomery, Joe Pass, Jim Hall, Pat Metheny, Joe Diorio), Byrdland; also, Borys, Epiphone, D'Angelico.

AMPS: Solid-state amps like the Roland JC-120 or Cube, Polytone Mini-Brute; or tube amps like the Fender Twin, Fender Bassman, and Matchless.

STRINGS: Some players favor heavier-gauged "flatwound" strings, producing a smoother, less-brassy tone. Guitars usually equipped with heavier strings, beginning with .011 to .013.

TONE TIPS: Use neck pickup of archtop hollowbody electric with tone knob rolled back slightly. Similar tone can be achieved by using the same approach with Gibson ES-335, Fender Telecaster, or Stratocaster.

ROCKABILLY/SWING

TONE CHARACTERISTICS: Hollowbody electric guitar played through an amp with a slight level of gain, and a touch of reverb and delay.

GUITARS: The king of modern rockabilly/swing, Brian Setzer, favors a '59 Gretsch 6120 Chet Atkins model guitar (equipped with a Bigsby tremolo); this is also the guitar Duane Eddy popularized.

AMPS: Setzer uses a pair of early-'60s Fender Bassmans (featuring Celestion Vintage 30-watt speakers), though any vintage Fender tube amp is suitable.

EFFECTS: "Slapback" echo, which can be created with any type of delay effect, is the key to achieving an effective rockabilly sound. Brian Setzer uses a Roland Model 301 Space Echo unit in conjunction with his '61 Fender reverb tank.

TONE TIPS: Whatever kind of guitar you have, plug it into a slightly distorted amp with your guitar's volume knob cranked, then turn the volume knob back until the sound loses most of its mush. If you have a Strat-style guitar, try experimenting with the middle or back pickups and your tone control knob until you're able to get a twangy but tolerable tone. If you have a digital delay, you can simulate rockabilly's slap echo effect by setting your unit at 100–150 ms (w/feedback and regeneration at "0").

SURF GUITAR

TONE CHARACTERISTICS: Fender guitars played with a grainy (i.e., slightly distorted) clean tone, soaked with reverb.

GUITARS: Fender Strats, Jazzmasters, and Jaguars.

AMPS: Vintage Fender tube amps (e.g., Showman, Twin, etc.) equipped with built-in spring reverb to achieve the characteristic "wet" sound.

EFFECTS: Many guitarists from the "surf" era used an external reverb tank manufactured by Fender, per Dick Dale's request.

STRINGS: Heavy gauge strings are preferred (Dick Dale uses .014).

TONE TIPS: To get a snappy tone reminiscent of most surf guitar performances, use a combination of treble and middle pickups.

RHYTHM RIFFS

ACCOMPANIMENT PATTERNS AND CHORD PROGRESSIONS FOR ANY STYLE

Let's say you're on the bandstand, and your fearless leader calls out a tune that you've never heard in your life. This is a common situation if you're subbing for a pal and have never played with this particular group of musicians. What would you do? Well, just as there are appropriate songs for certain type of gigs, there are generic riffs and chord-strumming patterns that instantly sound "right"—riffs that are unmistakably blues, country, funk, jazz, reggae/ska, or rock, for example. By having a couple of authentic-sounding accompaniment patterns for every style under your belt, you'll be able to "fake" your way through anything and live to play another day...

BLUES

FULLY-FRETTED/MOVABLE BOOGIE PATTERNS

Believe it or not, the most easily identifiable type of blues accompaniment actually has a name. It's called a *boogie pattern*—a guitaristic adaptation of the type of bluesy piano accompaniment associated with "boogie woogie" blues pianists. This style of accompaniment usually revolves around the familiar root/fifth power chord sonority, with additional chord tones (usually the 6th and ♭7th) performed in alternation with the chord's fifth. The overall effect implies a dominant seventh chord (e.g., "A7").

Below are two extremely common movable boogie patterns—in the user-friendly key of A—reminiscent of riffs played by artists ranging from T-Bone Walker, Chuck Berry, and Elvis, to the Beatles, Rolling Stones, and Led Zeppelin. Having a movable or "fully-fretted" version of this pattern at your disposal will enable to you fake your way through a blues tune in any key by simply moving the shape up or down the fretboard. All you need to do is target the root of each chord from a I–IV–V progression with your fret-hand's index finger and, provided you're working string pairs 4-5 or 5-6, plug in the shape. After learning each of the following riffs in A (the "I" chord), try transposing them to D (the "IV" chord) and E (the "V" chord). This will make it possible to play a complete blues in A.

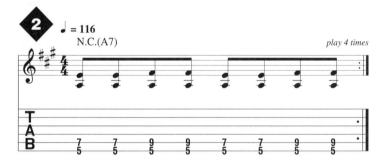

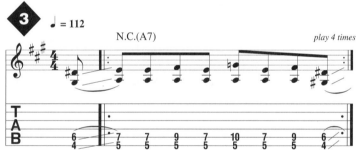

OPEN-POSITION BOOGIE PATTERNS

Movable boogie patterns definitely have versatility built into them. However, the fact that your fret-hand's index finger must consistently be anchored to each chord's root substantially limits the number of possible variations. By playing boogie patterns in the open position, relegating a chord's root to an open string, your index finger becomes freed up, enabling you to incorporate more embellishments (e.g., hammer-ons, pull-offs, slides) into a riff. Of course, this approach is only applicable to a limited number of chords—specifically, A, D, and E—because we have a limited number of open strings. In fact, "A" is the only key in which you can play a complete blues cycle using open-position boogie patterns exclusively. This is due to the fact that the guitar's bottom three strings correspond to the root notes of that key's I–IV–V progression. When playing a blues in other keys, most players will use a combination of movable and open-position patterns to suit their own individual tastes, or employ a capo.

Try transposing the following open-position boogie patterns, presented here in the key of A, to the remaining chords in an A blues. Next, try using them in an E blues (E, A, and B chords), using a movable pattern to imply the B chord. Note the use of "triplet feel," indicated over the notation staff in each of the following examples.

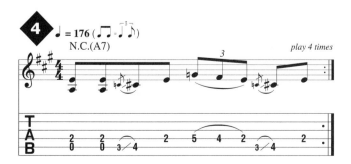

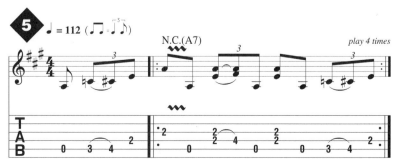

MINOR-KEY BOOGIE PATTERNS

Here's a question for you: What do you do if you have to play a blues in a minor key—where the previous riffs won't work due to their major key leanings—and strumming chords won't cut it? Answer: You bust out your minor-key boogie patterns!

Though the above described scenario is not nearly as common as the typical I–IV–V dominant seventh chord-based blues, rest assured it's out there. The following pair of fully fretted riffs are suitable for performance over most any minor blues. After you get these down, try transposing each of them to fit a few basic blues progressions in A minor: i–iv–v (Am–Dm–Em); i–iv–V (Am–Dm–E7#9); and i–iv–VI–V (Am–Dm–F–E7#9).

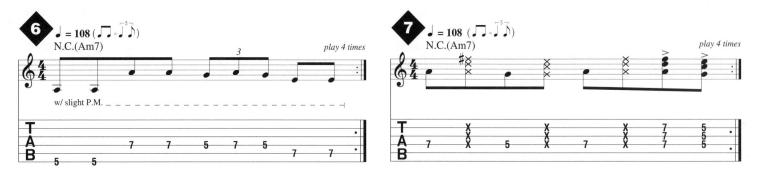

BLUES ACCOMPANIMENT IN AN R&B SETTING

Some gigs may require you to augment your blues repertoire with popular selections from a style like R&B. Not to worry. In most cases, blues-based rhythm guitar parts can also be utilized in this context. Try your hand at a few of the following figures, each of which is directly related to the movable A major barre chord form with the root on the sixth string.

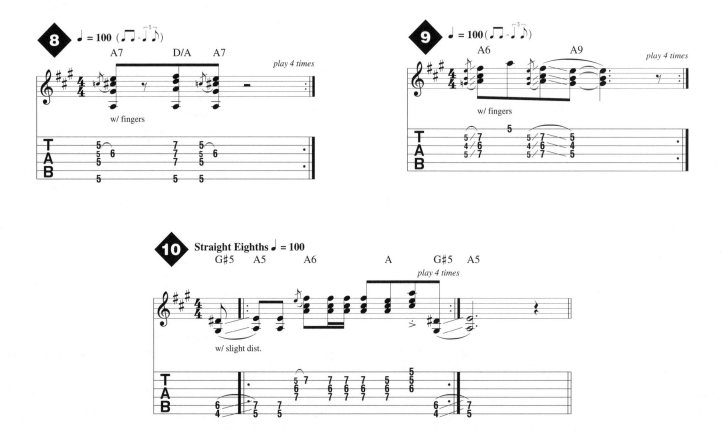

COUNTRY

ALTERNATING BASS PATTERNS WITH MELODIC EMBELLISHMENTS

In many country music formats, the guitar engages in a strumming style that combines two different elements: the alternation between a pair of bass notes (the root and fifth) played on beats 1 and 3, and chord strums on beats 2 and 4. This "country strum" is adaptable to both acoustic and electric instruments, and, because it creates the illusion of two different parts, fills in a lot of space. Melodic embellishments are also often incorporated into this strumming style—particularly when open-position chords are involved.

As you familiarize yourself with the following open-position chord patterns, keep in mind that many country guitarists, when changing keys to accommodate different vocalists, employ a capo when transposing. This enables them to use these same shapes to play in different keys (see p. 47 for more on how to use a capo to transpose).

Melodic embellishments can be taken to extremes in this style, to the point where there's a perceptible melodic line lurking within a strummed figure. This is a great way to supercharge your basic open-position chord shapes. The passage that follows features a melody confined to the guitar's lower strings, and eighth-note strums on the instrument's higher strings during beats 2 and 4 *á la* Doc Watson.

TRAVIS PICKING (OPEN-POSITION PATTERNS)

Another timeless type of country accompaniment involves a quasi-fingerstyle approach referred to as *Travis picking*. This style was popularized by country guitar virtuoso Merle Travis, and involves playing alternating bass notes with the thumb of your right hand (or a thumbpick), while plucking melodic parts with the remaining fingers of your right hand.

The next several examples depict a wide variety of Travis picking possibilities, using common open-position chords: B7, E7, A7, D7/F#, G7, C7, and F. Notice that the aforementioned chords were listed in "cycle of fifths" order, yielding a continually modulating V–I cadence. Once you get comfortable with each two-bar pattern, try linking them together, playing them all in succession. For an even greater challenge, try plugging each two-bar figure (without taking the repeats) into a series of different chord progressions like: C7–F–C7–G7; G7–C7–G7–D7/F#; D7/F#–G7–D7/F#–A7; A7–D7/F#–A7–E7; E7–A7–E7–B7. With a little practice, you'll eventually be able to improvise in the Travis picking style, within the confines of each open-position chord shape. And don't forget: you can also use a capo to change keys.

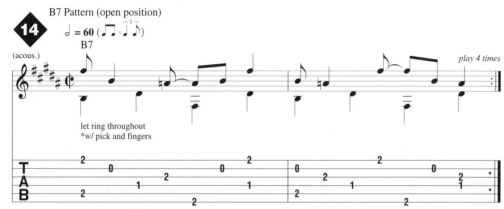

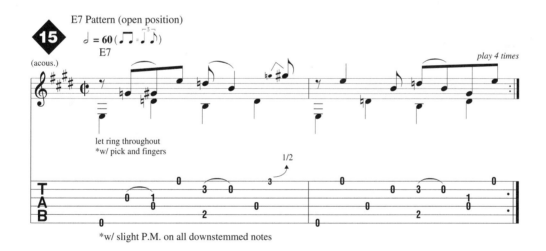

D7 Pattern (open position)

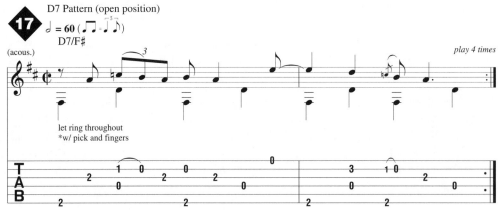

let ring throughout
*w/ pick and fingers

*w/ slight P.M. on all downstemmed notes.

G7 Pattern (open position)

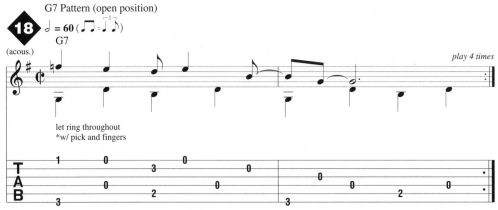

let ring throughout
*w/ pick and fingers

*w/ slight P.M. on all downstemmed notes.

C7 Pattern (open position)

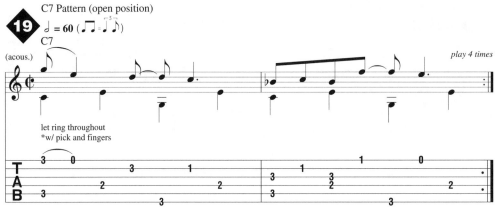

let ring throughout
*w/ pick and fingers

*w/ slight P.M. on all downstemmed notes.

F Pattern (open position)

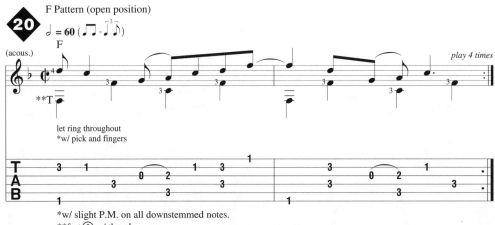

let ring throughout
*w/ pick and fingers

*w/ slight P.M. on all downstemmed notes.
**fret ⑥ w/ thumb

TRAVIS PICKING (FULLY-FRETTED/MOVABLE VERSIONS)

So what happens if you need to play a country tune that involves a nondiatonic (outside of the key) chord? What if a modulation to a different key occurs, making open-position shapes off limits? In order to use your familiar open-position shapes to accommodate the new chord, midway through the tune, you might have to stop playing and slap on a capo—or, even worse, if you're already capoed up, stop playing for a second and move your capo. Reality check: Unless you drank six gallons of coffee prior to taking the stage, that approach will never work. For such a situation, with an arsenal of fully fretted Travis picking patterns—figures relating to common, movable barre chord shapes—you'll have enough ammo to pull off the uncommon chord change.

The four figures to the right illustrate various two-measure Travis-picking patterns within the framework of fully fretted dominant seventh chord shapes. For maximum flexibility, the shapes are presented in different "root on sixth string" and "root on fifth string" formats. Once you learn each shape in its respective position, try moving it to different positions to imply different chords. For example: After playing the G7 shape in the third position, move it verbatim up to the eighth fret to imply a C7 chord (the "IV" chord), then the tenth position to imply a D7 chord (the "V" chord). Learn each of the following shapes in the same manner, until you can nail the I–IV–V changes in the keys of E, A, D, and G. In the end, you'll likely be equipped to make your way through a basic I–IV–V country progression in any key. You'll also develop some serious Travis-picking chops! As is the case with most accompaniment patterns, try to become equally comfortable performing these types of figures on both acoustic and electric instruments.

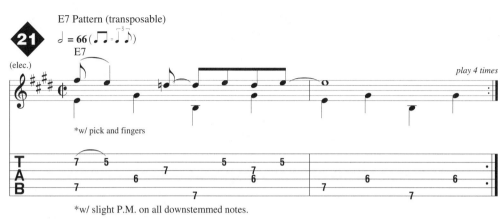

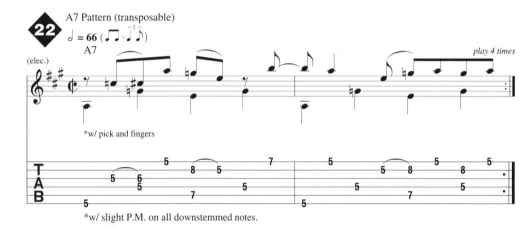

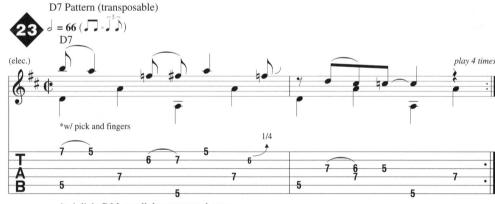

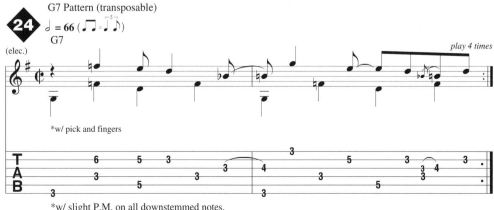

FUNK

GROOVING ON DOMINANT SEVENTH CHORD SHAPES

At some point during a given gig, somebody will decide that it's time to "get the funk out." Familiarizing yourself with funky strumming patterns (reminiscent of Jimmy Nolan's rhythm work with James Brown, for example) will pay off in a big way. A typical Nolan-style funk guitar part is characterized by relentless sixteenth-note scratches, offset with syncopated chord stabs from the dominant seventh family (E7, E9, E7#9, etc.). These chord stabs are often either synchronized with the band's horn section or used to fill in the cracks left behind by the other musicians' parts. The bottom line is that the guitar's role is more rhythmic and percussive than harmonic. When tackling the following figure, keep your strumming hand loose, rotating it at the wrist as you alternate between down- and upstrokes.

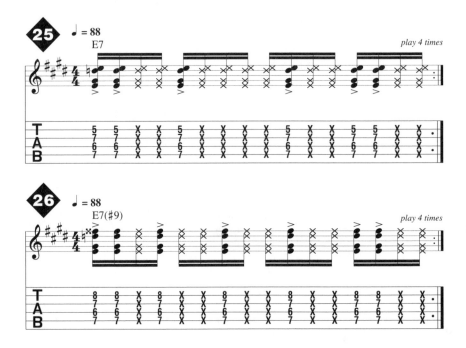

This next figure is played with a sixteenth-note swing feel. This approach to interpreting funky rhythms is often referred to as New Jack Swing, or "swunk" (short for "swing-funk"). If you're unfamiliar with this bouncy feel, use the provided audio source as a guide. Your ears will definitely be familiar with this type of funk groove.

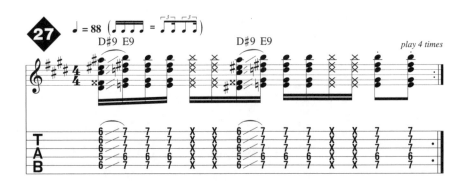

FUNKY CHORD PARTIALS

In funk, chord partials are also frequently used to juice up a guitar part. These types of two- or three-note sonorities add more meat to a riff, oftentimes harmonizing a single-note figure in the process.

Overall, the first of the following two figures implies an E7#9 sound. The second figure is more appropriate for minor-key funk, as it implies an Em7 chord and is rooted in E Dorian (E–F♯–G–A–B–C♯–D).

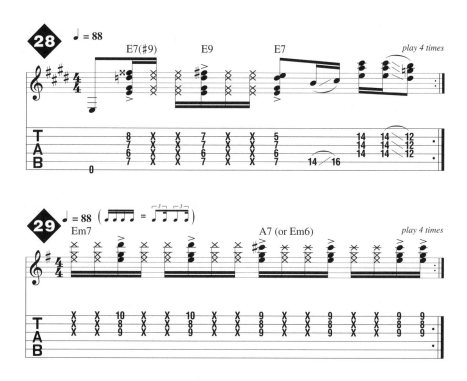

FUNKY SINGLE-NOTE RIFFS

Single-note riffs are also a common characteristic of funk. These types of passages often involve tricky syncopations, and include everything from muted notes and double stops to phrasing devices like hammer-ons, pull-offs, slides, and string bends. Most guitarists who play funk choose to add extra grit to these types of riffs by aggressively smacking the majority of the guitar's strings while using fret-hand muting to dampen the adjacent strings, allowing only the intended notes to ring out. These funk figures are frequently treated with effects like wah-wah, phase shifter, and envelope filter, and are occasionally doubled an octave lower by the bass guitar.

This first pair of single-note funk figures occurs in the fifth position, and involves pitches from either A minor pentatonic (A–C–D–E–G) or A Dorian (A–B–C–D–E–F♯–G). Of course, since these riffs involve fretted notes exclusively, they can easily be moved to accommodate any other key. Try playing both of these funk riffs using your fret-hand's thumb to grab the root on the sixth string (*á la* Jimi Hendrix). For maximum funkiness, employ a wah-wah pedal, rocking your foot to the treble position with each beat (just like you're tapping your foot).

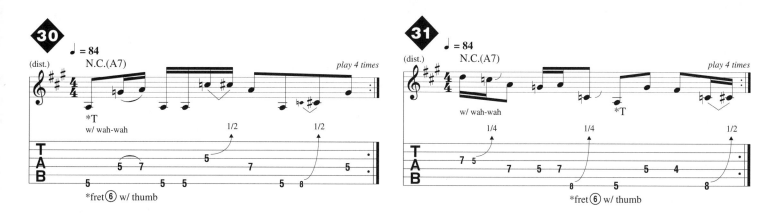

These next two single-note funk figures also revolve around A minor pentatonic and A Dorian sounds. The first one involves legato fret-hand slides, achieving an interesting phrasing effect. The latter is performed in fixed position, and uses a variety of legato techniques including pull-offs and fret-hand slides. It's also treated with a psychedelic phase-shifting effect. For best results, allow these notes to ring together as much as possible.

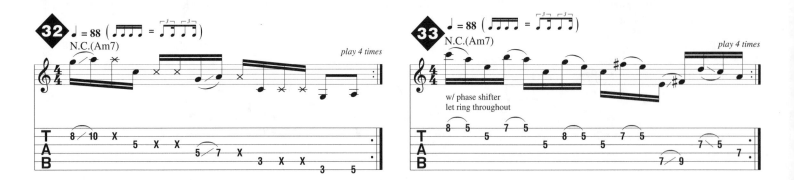

FULL-BLOWN FUNK

Combining all of the aforementioned elements—chords, chord partials, and single notes—can yield some impressive funk riffs. Here are a few fixed-position funk figures to freak out your friends!

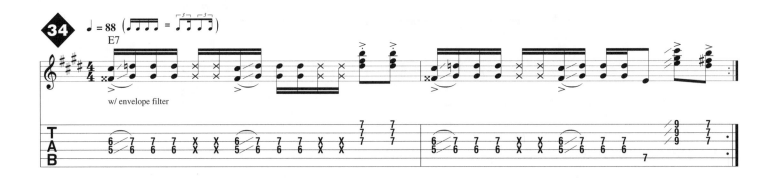

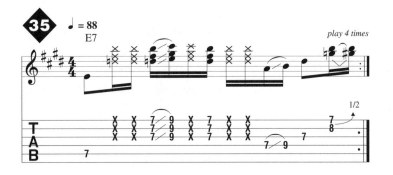

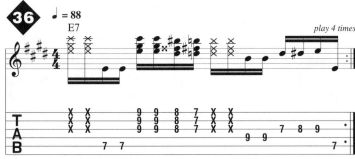

18

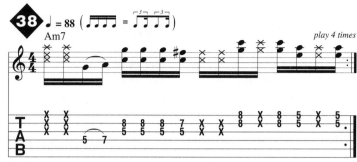

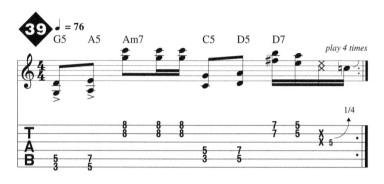

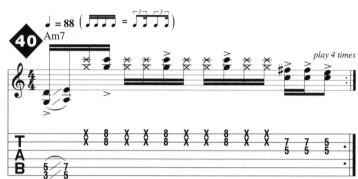

JAZZ

ROOT-POSITION "JAZZ" CHORDS IN II–V–I PROGRESSIONS

At the core of any jazz tune lies a cyclic arrangement of colorful "jazz chords"—like the minor seventh, dominant seventh, and major seventh. This means that having a limited arsenal of run-of-the-mill major and minor barre chords just won't cut it if your piano player pulls out the Real Book (a 400+ page book containing jazz standards) and starts counting off a tune. Instead, you'll need to have some seventh chords under your fingers—and the ability to play them in a ii-V-I progression in a variety of keys.

The figures that follow illustrate several different ii-V-I progressions in the key of C. They make use of *voice leading* (minimal movement between notes as chords change) and *extended chords* (e.g., minor ninth, dominant thirteenth, and major ninth chords). Each of the shapes appearing in this first section are performed in "root position," meaning that the chord's root is the lowest sounding note. In some instances, the altered tones used to color G7 are taken to extremes using *tritone substitution*—superimposing a triad that occurs the interval of a tritone away (in this case, D♭) over a fixed root. In general, alterations can be applied to a dominant seventh chord any time it is used as a "V" chord in a V–I cadence. Use a clean amp setting, and back off your guitar's tone knob to achieve the characteristic warmth of a real hollowbody electric jazz guitar.

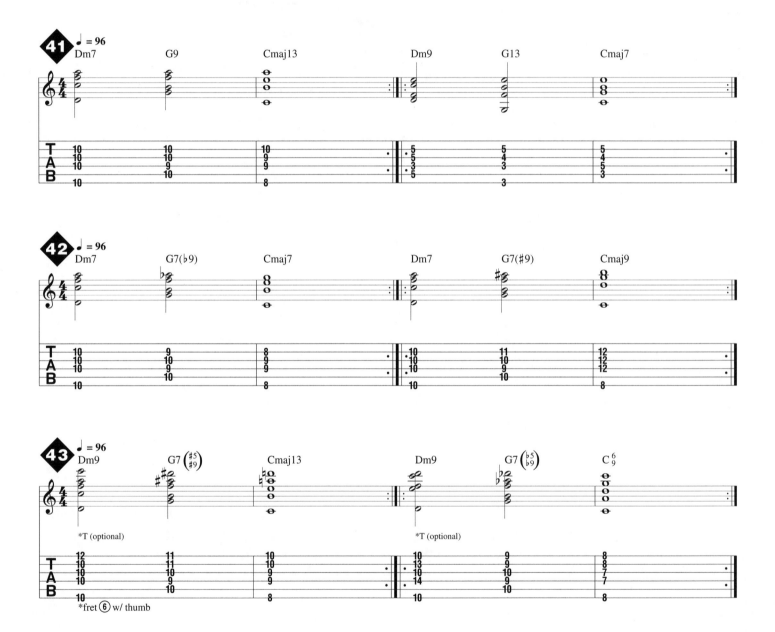

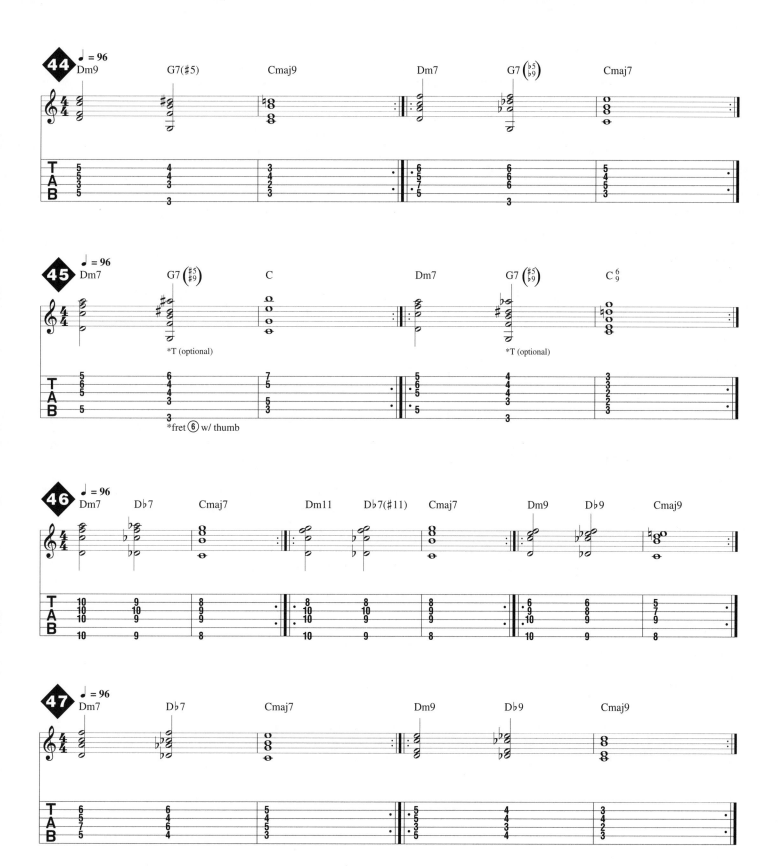

CHORD MELODY PRIMER

As you no doubt discovered from running your fingers through the previous ii–V–I examples, there are several different variations for each type of "root position" chord. Take, for example, the different variations of Dm7 found at the fifth fret. Though these shapes share the same "D" bass note, the highest notes often vary from voicing to voicing. Using any combination of the Dm7 chords you just learned, try alternating randomly between them, focusing your ear on the highest note found in each chord. Notice that the fluctuation in pitches on the higher strings creates melodic activity. This approach is the basis for what's referred to as "chord melody"—playing chords and melody simultaneously. Getting a handle on this "solo jazz guitar" approach will save your hide if you need to whip off a piano-style intro on the spot.

The following ii–V–I example involves the performance of several different chord shapes per chord type. As the bass note for each chord remains stationary, the different voicings force you to play a variety of pitches along the second string, creating a melodic line.

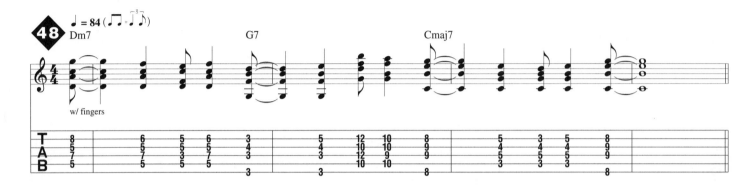

CHORD MELODY USING INVERSIONS

Of course, using strictly root position chords immediately limits the melodic complexity of your chord solos. But by using chord extensions and mastering a variety of inversions—so thoroughly that you can use their highest-sounding notes to outline an ascending or descending scale of any type—your only limitation becomes your own imagination.

This next pair of examples follows a ii–V–I progression in C, using a combination of inversions and chord extensions to create melodic movement along the first and second strings. Notice the "stacked fourth" shapes used to imply Cmaj7 in some instances.

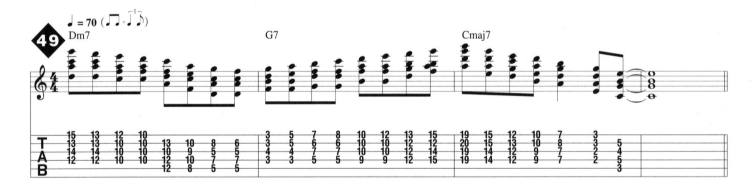

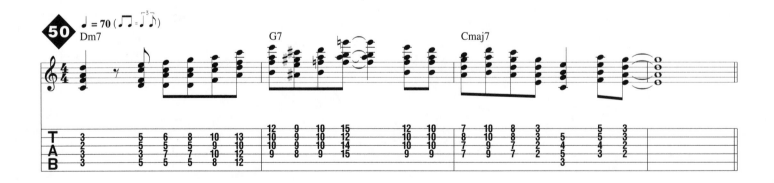

TWO-NOTE VOICINGS

Virtually any of the voicings you just learned will sound right at home in a large jazz ensemble. They'll even work in a trio setting, provided you're the only harmonic instrument (i.e., no piano in the group). But in instances where you're playing a jazz gig as a quartet—with guitar, piano, bass, and drums—you'll most likely want to stay out of the harmonic range of the piano player. For that reason, you'll need to "trim down" some of your chord voicings. This can be done simply by eliminating the root and fifth of each chord, using strictly thirds and sevenths to imply the harmony. In a ii–V–I progression in C, the notes you'll want to grab will be: F and C (♭3 and 7) for Dm7, B and F (3 and ♭7) for G7, and E and B (3 and 7) for Cmaj7. Check out the smooth voice leading (with each note moving no more than a half step) that results from using only thirds and sevenths in the following ii–V–I cycle.

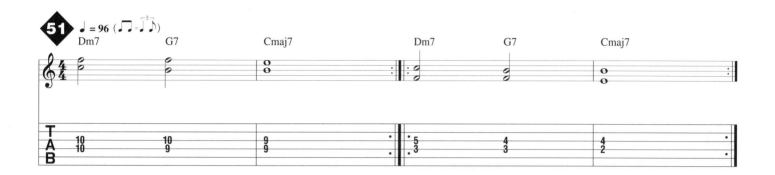

Since these sparse voicings only require—at most—two fret-hand fingers to execute, it becomes quite simple to interject melody into an accompaniment figure. Notice the chromatic line that results from placing extensions and alterations along the first string in each of the following pair of ii–V–I–VI examples. By using a familiar comping rhythm beneath this melodic line, you can create the illusion of two different parts: melody and chordal accompaniment. These can be played using a variety of techniques: fingerstyle, pick and fingers, or pickstyle.

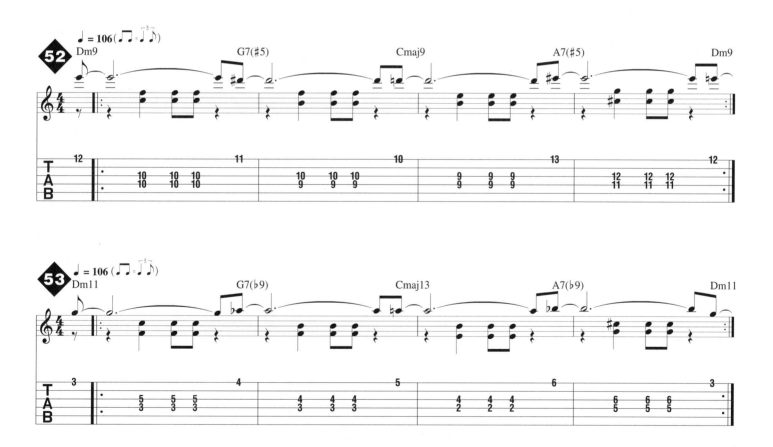

DISSONANT CHORD CLUSTERS

In the event you're hired for a "modern jazz" gig, you may find it worthwhile to familiarize yourself with some hipper voicings. By squeezing a chord's ninth in between a "thirds and sevenths" shape, you instantly arrive at some ultra-modern, beautifully dissonant chord clusters. The following "cluster voicing" examples outline a ii–V–I–vi progression. Notice how hip these voicings sound with a little rhythmic ingenuity, as depicted in the latter example.

MINOR II⁰-V-I CHORD PATTERNS

Practicing the ii⁰-V-i progression in a bunch of minor keys will also introduce new chord shapes into your seventh chord vocabulary. The following figures depict a minor ii⁰–V–i progression in the key of C minor, yielding a variety of minor 7♭5 and altered dominant shapes. Notice that everything from rudimentary chord-melody moves to permutations of the tonic minor chord [e.g., Cm6, Cm(maj7)] is woven into these examples. Most of these figures are also strummed in steady quarter notes, with accents occurring on beats 2 and 4.

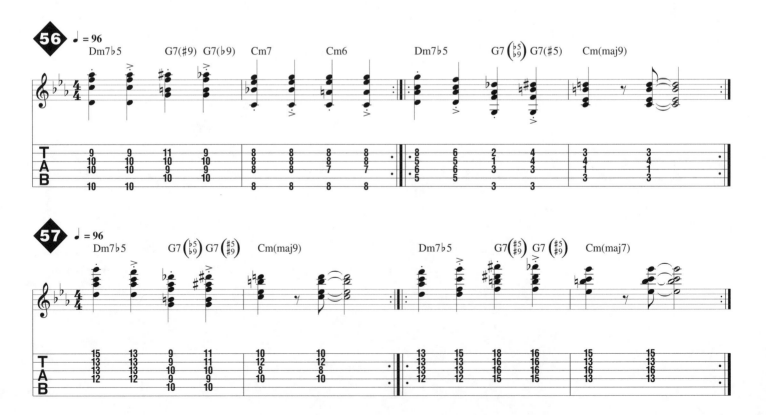

TEN ESSENTIAL COMPING RHYTHMS

Now that you've run yourself through the "jazz chord" wringer, try plugging any combination of chord voicings used in this chapter into some of the following rhythmic motifs. These ten essential rhythms constitute many of the characteristic comping patterns in jazz.

RHYTHM 'N' BLUES (A.K.A. R&B)

Hands down, rhythm 'n' blues is one of the most widely covered genres of popular music. Whether you're onstage paying tribute to Otis Redding with a rendition of "(Sittin' On) The Dock of the Bay," or plowing through a bunch of early-'80s Michael Jackson tunes at a hoppin' dance club, you're going to have to be able to "bust a groove" with your guitar to play in the R&B style. If your goal is to sound "authentic" when performing in these circles, familiarity with the soulful rhythm guitar work of '60s Stax Records icon Steve Cropper, as well as a host of '80s session heavyweights, is key.

'60S R&B

When it comes to getting a characteristic '60s R&B groove going, nothing sounds more authentic than Crop bustin'! During the '60s, guitarist Steve Cropper's classic riffs helped create a slew of classic R&B cuts: "Soul Man," "(Sittin' On) The Dock of the Bay," and "Knock On Wood," among several others. Playing primarily a Fender Telecaster through vintage tube amps, Cropper carved out his signature rhythm guitar style by combining driving single-note riffs with strategically placed two- and three-note chord stabs reminiscent of horn-section punches.

The following figure revolves around a variety of three-note voicings, implying an A7 tonality, plugged into a patented Steve Cropper rhythm guitar template. To properly cop Cropper's feel, take note of the staccato chord phrasings that occur on the fourth beat of each measure. At these instances, you should relax your fret-hand's grip immediately after smacking the indicated strings. Also notice the frequent occurrence of the familiar bluesy hammer-ons from C (5th fret, 3rd string) to C♯ (6th fret, 3rd string) on beat 1 and the "and" of 2. This soulful rhythm guitar motif is yet another signature Cropperism!

'80S POP-INFLUENCED R&B

If you plan on paying your bills by playing gigs with a "dance-pop" band, you're going to need to get intimate with a lot of pop-influenced R&B records from the '80s—many of which contain burning rhythm guitar parts played by top-notch session guitarists! Taking their cues from the groove masters of the '60s (Curtis Mayfield), '70s (session ace Lee Ritenour), and early '80s (Prince), players like Paul Jackson Jr. and David Williams carved out their own niche in the '80s by contributing most of that era's signature rhythm guitar parts. By similarly copping tasty licks from a wide range of sources, with practice, you'll be able to "play in the pocket" like the pros!

This next example incorporates several characteristics of an '80s pop-influenced R&B guitar part: soulful double-stop hammer-ons/pull-offs, slightly palm-muted single-note riffs (referred to as "popcorn picking," in some circles), and pentatonic licks.

Incidentally, if your band's goal is to accurately recreate all the glossy glitz of '80s synth-pop production, you'll undoubtedly have a keyboard player in the lineup who's playing through a big rack of synth gear. You may even be playing along with preprogrammed tracks! For this reason, many "modern" R&B guitarists favor the high-endy, percussive tone that a Strat-style guitar offers, using either the bridge-and-middle or neck-and-middle pickups (on clean parts) to cut through the density of synthesized sounds.

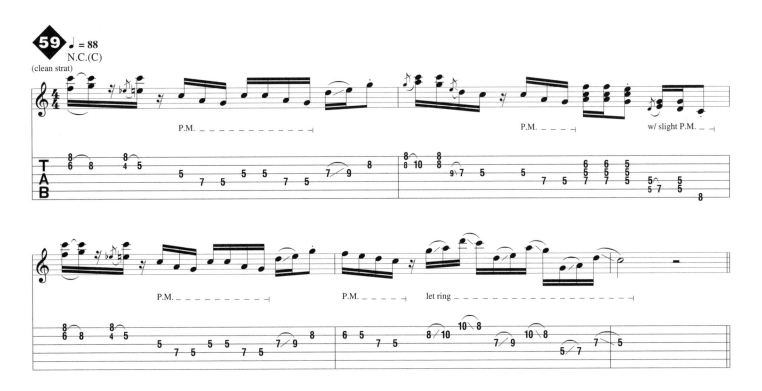

REGGAE AND SKA

Reggae and ska are two other musical styles you must also be prepared to cover. Why? Because, even if your bandleader says, "We're just gonna be playing a bunch of pop tunes," reality dictates that he or she will inevitably call off a pop tune that—despite the fact that it was performed by a "pop" artist—actually incorporates all the rhythmic elements of reggae or ska. (A short list of reggae/ska-inflected pop tunes would have to include Eric Clapton's "I Shot the Sheriff," Blondie's "The Tide is High," Paul Simon's "Mother and Child Reunion," and Stevie Wonder's "Master Blaster.") Not to put any more pressure on you, but a key characteristic of reggae and ska's overall vibe lies in the hands of the guitar player: three- or four-note voicings played right smack on beats 2 and 4 (in reggae) or on the "and" of each beat (in ska). These chords are usually played *staccato*—deliberately cutting short the ringing duration of each chord by "choking" the strings—using a clean amp setting.

REGGAE: THE "DROP"

Reggae is a somewhat moodier form of Jamaican music than ska. This "moody" vibe owes much to a laid-back groove, with harmonic content derived from minor chords. The following figure features chord strums on beats 2 and 4. In reggae, this strict rhythmic placement of chords is referred to as the "drop."

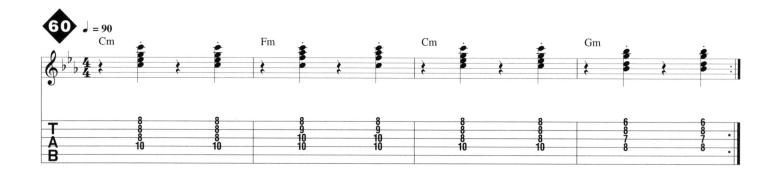

SKA: THE "SKANK"

In general, ska is more lively and upbeat than reggae. Therefore, ska-based chord progressions commonly revolve around major chords, and the tempo is rather quick. This next figure depicts a rudimentary ska rhythm guitar part, with a snapping upstroke "skank" used on the "and" of each beat.

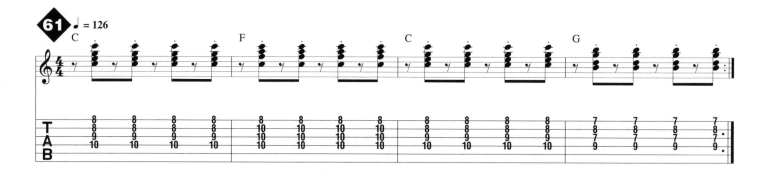

If any of the previous three- and four-note voicings seem as though they might be hard to remember, keep in mind that you can get by with simply strumming the highest strings of a garden-variety barre chord. Also, if you find yourself on the bandstand playing a reggae/ska tune you've never heard, direct your ears towards your bass player's simple and repetitive bass line, and double his or her part, note for note. This will provide you with an instantly cool variation to whip out during less dynamically intense moments.

ROCK

HENDRIX-STYLE ACCOMPANIMENT

In classic rock, R&B, and pop, there are several ways to create a happening rhythm guitar part without having to rely upon strumming garden-variety barre chords. One of the hippest ways to do this is by using pentatonic-based chord partials *à la* Jimi Hendrix or Curtis Mayfield in place of standard chord structures. In general, these types of "Hendrix-y" fills involve playing two or more neighboring strings simultaneously (sticking to the appropriate pentatonic pitches) and allowing them to ring together as much as possible. These types of rhythm guitar figures are most effective when used to fill in behind a vocal phrase or to spruce up an instrumental section.

In the two following examples, pentatonic scales are superimposed over a "harmonically static" situation—that is, numerous consecutive measures in either C or C minor. When faced with this type of scenario, try using this simple rule of thumb: Always play major pentatonic scales over major chords (e.g., C major pentatonic, C–D–E–G–A, over a C chord), and minor pentatonic scales over minor chords (e.g., C minor pentatonic, C–Eb–F–G–Bb, over a Cm chord). Pentatonic scales can also be embellished upon by incorporating the "sus4" (the note "F" in C or Cm) or the "sus2/add9" (the note "D" in C or Cm) into the texture, and resolving them to the third (E or Eb) or root (C).

*fret ⑥ w/ thumb   *fret ⑥ w/ thumb

Incidentally, one of the easiest ways to introduce these types of figures into your rhythm guitar vocabulary is to "attach" a convenient pentatonic shape to every basic barre chord shape (based upon the same root) that you know. This will enable you to "file" these types of fills away for easy recall, since you're likely already adept at grabbing a variety of barre chords. The chord frames depicted over the previous examples should help you get started with the visualization process.

Once you get comfortable playing the previous figures, try this as an exercise. Strum the chord for two beats, then try improvising using pentatonic-based fill-ins. Eventually, you'll be able to improvise using this approach, providing you with a creative point of departure from garden-variety barre chords.

MODERN ROCK CHORD VOICINGS

In modern rock, another approach to chord manipulation is often explored. In many instances, garden-variety open-position "cowboy" chords are replaced with more colorful-sounding chords featuring extensions (e.g., sevenths, ninths, elevenths, and thirteenths) and/or suspensions (e.g., sus2 and sus4). In the following chord chart, various pitches are added to standard major and minor chords to produce more "modern-sounding" voicings, while still maintaining the requisite open-string jangle.

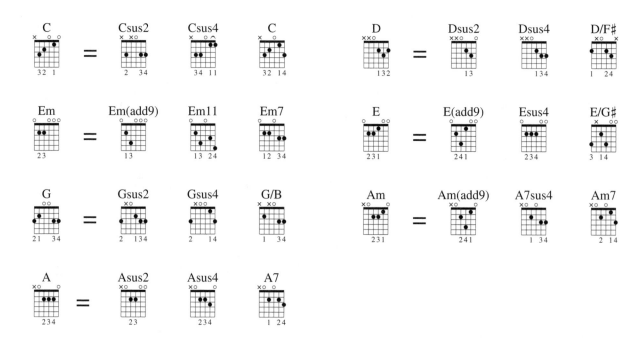

Basic barre chords can also be spruced up with the simple addition of chord suspensions and extensions.

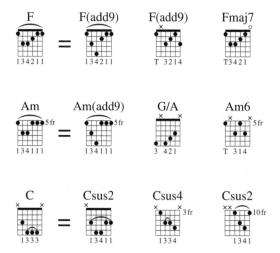

The following example combines both approaches—open-position chords and barre chords—in a typical modern rock progression, performed by two guitars. Like many contemporary rock productions, the acoustic guitar in this example is reserved for open-position strumming, providing percussive color, while an electric plays power chords and suspended shapes, interjecting rock techniques like palm-muting, arpeggiation, harmonics, and vibrato-bar dives into the soundscape.

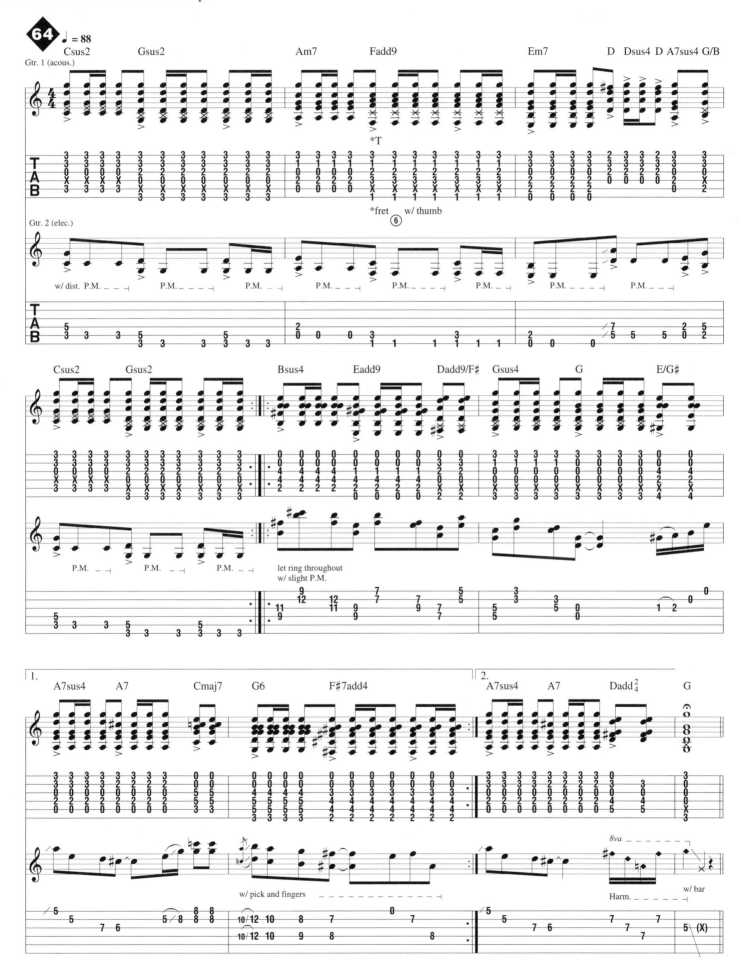

HEAVY METAL

Like any musical style, the popularity of heavy metal ebbs and flows. Be that as it may, it seems every town—dating back to the early '70s—has always had someone carrying the heavy metal torch. Whether the gospel of metal is being spread via a Black Sabbath-, Deep Purple-, or Led Zeppelin-inspired "classic metal" tribute band, or an '80s "glam-metal" cover band resurrecting the music of Mötley Crüe, Quiet Riot, or Ratt, the effectiveness of the "tribute" lies in the guitar player's hands. Why? Because riffs are what metal is all about—the metallic sound of a solidbody guitar run through a heavily distorted Marshall, punishing listeners with ominous-sounding power chords and percussive, palm-muted, open-string drones. Even if you've never played metal before, by boning up on these types of "industry standard" metal characteristics, you'll be ahead of the game when it comes time to churn out the chunk like a full-fledged metalhead.

The following "classic metal"-inspired riff—a cross between late-'60s/early-'70s British metal and late-'70s/early-'80s European metal—combines power chords and other dyads (two-note chord partials) with the occasional single-note riff, all interspersed amongst a healthy dose of the genre's obligatory palm-muted open Es. Incidentally, this riff also occurs in heavy metal's most common key, E Aeolian minor (E–F#–G–A–B–C–D), though the exotic mode of E Phrygian (E–F–G–A–B–C–D) is implied in the final bar with the implementation of a nondiatonic chord, F5.

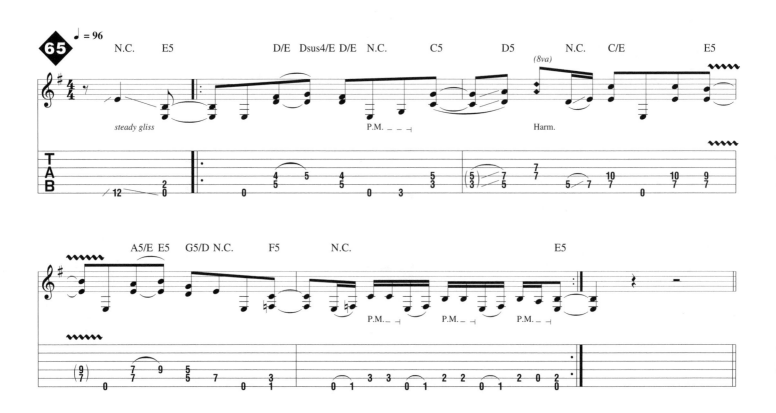

GRUNGE

What happens when you combine sledgehammer-like guitar sounds with unpredictable meter changes, oddball tunings, and a dose of punk rock angst—all played on "pawn shop" guitars through a stripped-down amp setup? Answer: Grunge. With the massive popularity grunge enjoyed in the early '90s—as epitomized by bands like Soundgarden, Nirvana, Alice in Chains, and Pearl Jam—it's inevitable that, at some point, you'll have to unload the "Seattle sound" on your paying customers.

In the early '90s, one significant trait shared between grunge acts was the use of Drop D tuning (low to high: D–A–D–G–B–E). This tuning was a particular favorite among guitarists like Kim Thayil (Soundgarden) and Jerry Cantrell (Alice in Chains). By simply lowering the pitch of the guitar's sixth string one whole step from E to D (you can find this pitch by detuning the sixth string's twelfth fret harmonic to match the pitch of the open fourth string), "one-finger" power chords become possible. This "single-digit" demand on your fret hand not only makes it a piece of cake to move power chords all over the neck, it also makes it possible to shift between shapes using hammer-ons/pull-offs, or to interject a disturbing-sounding power-chord string bend by yanking the shape across the neck! Toss in a few odd metrical shifts (e.g., from 4/4 to 7/8 or 5/8), and you'll sound like a true Seattle native.

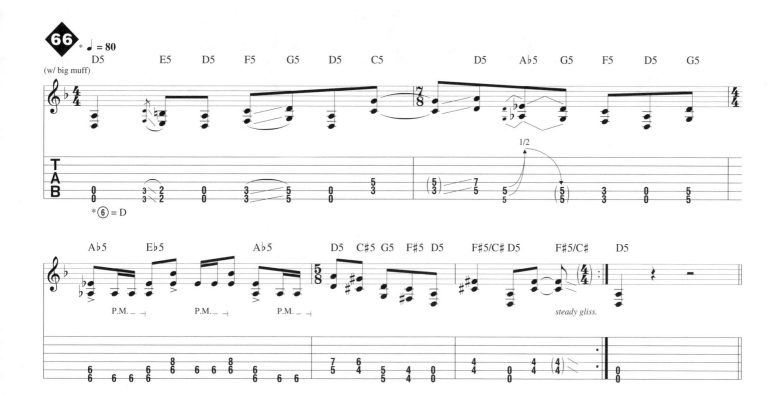

LEAD LICKS

BUILDING A VOCABULARY FOR SOLOS, FILLS, AND MORE

Imagine your bandleader points to you midway through whatever song you're playing. What could that mean? Well, chances are, unless the song is "Happy Birthday" and they're giving you a surprise honor, it probably means it's time for an impromptu guitar solo! And if you don't have a reasonable number of licks that sound "in the style," you may wish that you never took your guitar out of its case!

Licks are musical phrases that can be used in a soloing context, to "fill in" behind the singer's vocal phrases, or to dress up the end of a tune. The guitar is frequently the instrument that fills in—particularly in blues, country, jazz, and rock styles. Try learning as many licks as you can in every conceivable style until they become second nature and you can whip 'em out at will. An added bonus of having a versatile vocabulary of licks is that if you and your band members are good improvisers, you can stretch out the length of your songs, meaning you can "survive" with fewer songs in your set.

BLUES

TURNAROUNDS

A *turnaround* is a kind of lick that's used to fill in at the end of the 12-bar blues form, prompting the band to "turn around" and go back to the beginning of the form.

In the following blues turnaround, a chromatically descending arrangement of sixths is articulated using a combination of pick and fingers (measure 1), while an E9 chord—the V chord in an A blues—puts the cap on it in the final measure. Notice that the E9 chord is preceded from one half step above (the distance of one fret) with an F9 chord. This half-step movement into the V chord—approaching it from above or below—is a common characteristic of most blues turnarounds.

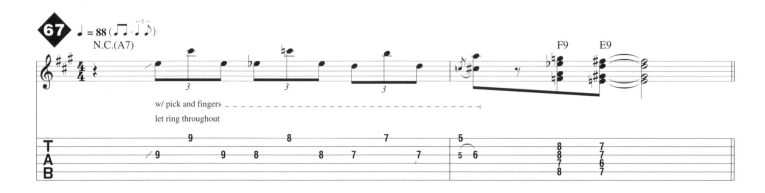

Other versions of blues turnarounds can be created using approaches like double stops and arpeggiation, as well as phrasing devices like bending and hammer-ons/pull-offs. Here are a few turnarounds using different combinations of the aforementioned techniques. Notice that each of them uses chromaticism in one form or another—in a single-note, double-stop, or chord context.

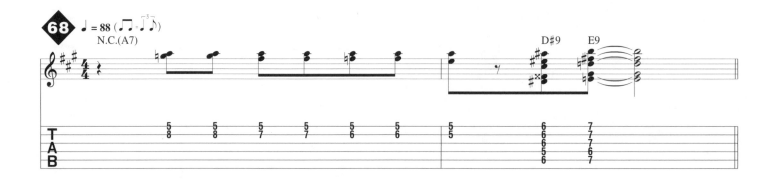

TAGS

How many times have you jammed on a blues tune with your buddies and not been able to bring the song to an effective conclusion? With a few tags in your bag of licks, this problem will cease to exist.

A *tag* is a musical phrase that's usually executed by the person playing the final solo in a number, signifying the end of the song. Play through the following E minor pentatonic (E–G–A–B–D) blues tag, gradually slowing down its tempo as you work your way towards the closing chord (E9). Remember: All eyes will be on you at this point—it's your job to cue the band. And the crowd goes wild!

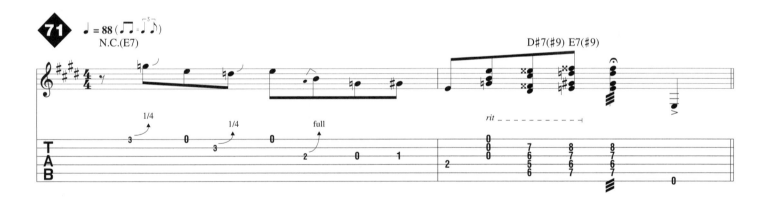

Of course, just as we encountered with turnarounds, tags can also be varied using double stops, microtonal bends, and the like. Run your fingers through these next three blues tags, adapt them to other keys, and then try creating some of your own.

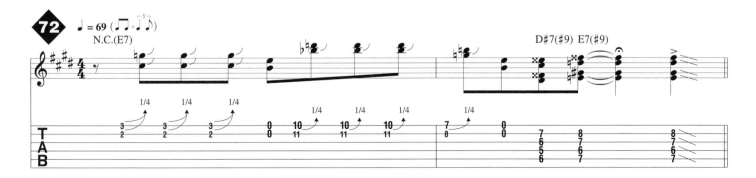

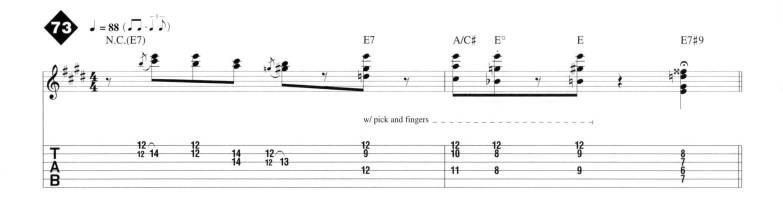

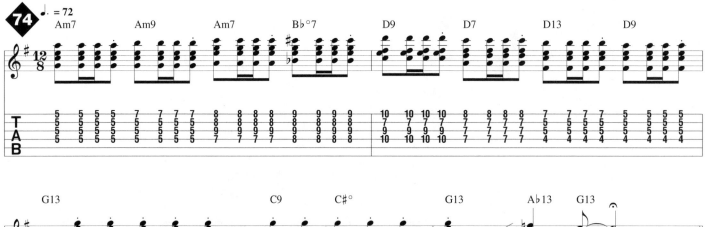

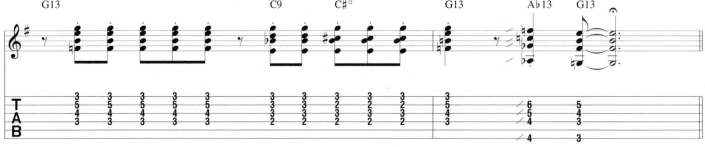

TIMELESS CLICHÉS

In any form of music, certain melodic fragments sound more at home than others. This is particularly true of blues music. If you were to "drop the needle" on a Robert Johnson record made in the '30s, chances are you'd hear many motifs that are still being used by today's blues vocalists and instrumentalists—timeless blues clichés that have survived for generations. This is representative of the "blues tradition": the act of passing down musical motifs from player to player, over the span of decades. In short, whether you're listening to blues players like Muddy Waters, T-Bone Walker, B.B. King, Buddy Guy, Lonnie Mack, Eric Clapton, or Stevie Ray Vaughan, it's a given that you'll hear some melodic common ground. The same holds true for blues-based rockers like Jeff Beck, Jimi Hendrix, and Jimmy Page.

In blues at its most basic, minor and major pentatonic licks are considered "industry standard." These licks are typically phrased using fret-hand pitch bends ranging from microtonal (e.g., 1/4 step) to a minor third (1-1/2 step), fret-hand vibrato oscillating at a speed and width that's not too excessive, typical legato techniques such as hammer-ons/pull-offs/slides, and lots of dynamics.

The following figures depict a wide variety of classic blues phrases, sounding exclusively in E minor pentatonic (E–G–A–B–D). In each example, notice that different licks are labeled over the notation staff as motifs A–D, but performed in succession to create a four-bar phrase. After you learn each example as written and you're able to play along with the accompanying recording, isolate each individual motif and repeat it, sing it aloud, and transpose it to other keys—whatever is necessary to help you implant that phrase into your musical memory. Then, for a musical exercise, put on your favorite blues record and try to play back each phrase you hear (vocal or instrumental) immediately after the artist performs it. Think of this as an artificial "call-and-response" scenario. Another similar approach might be to listen exhaustively to one blues solo (away from your instrument) until you can sing it back, then attempt playing it along with the record on the fly—without transcribing it in advance. Before long, you'll be able to hear these motifs in your head and improvise a tasty blues solo, "off the cuff," like a real bluesman/blueswoman!

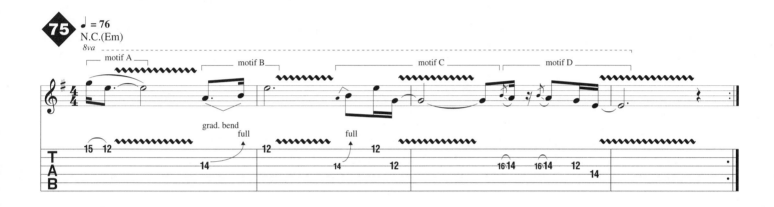

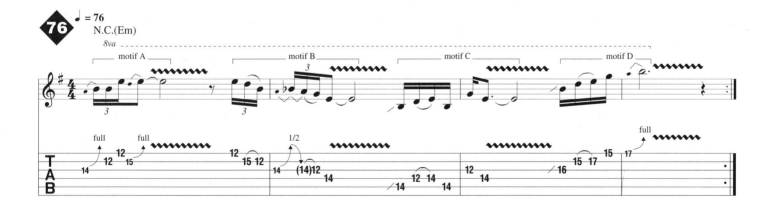

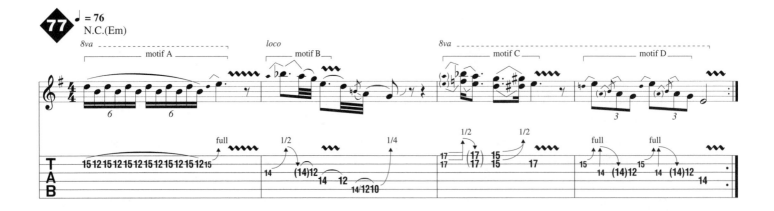

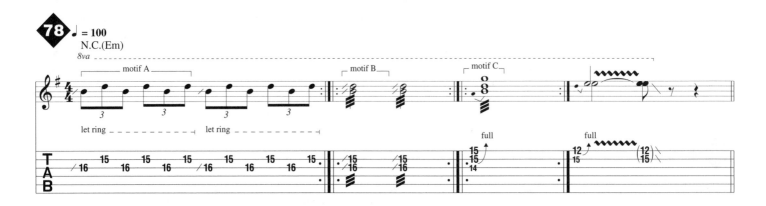

Here's another handful of common blues phrases, grouped as motifs A–C, this time appearing in E major pentatonic (E–F♯–G♯–B–C♯). Practice these in the same manner you did the previous examples, then experiment with alternating between or blending together both minor pentatonic and major pentatonic scales over a static E7 chord. Keep a mental note of the effect each different scale creates, with the goal of developing a sense of tension (minor pentatonic) and resolution (major pentatonic) produced when you fluctuate between the two scale sounds over the same chord.

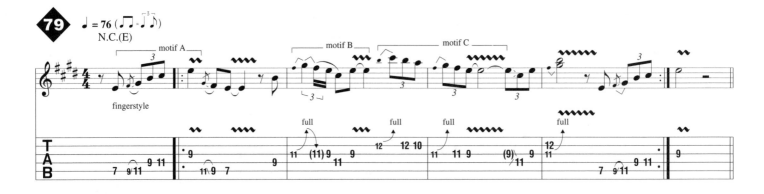

This last blues lick blurs the line between E major pentatonic and E minor pentatonic scales. It also incorporates some chromaticism along the high string.

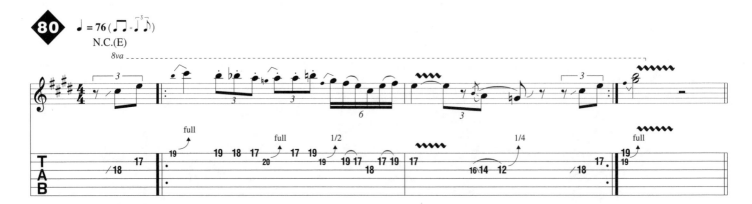

COUNTRY

OPEN-POSITION SINGLE-NOTE LICKS

In country music, there are tons of cliché, open-position licks that are equally appropriate for performance on either acoustic or electric guitar. Generally, these types of licks are performed over an implied dominant seventh chord harmony, providing improvisers with a host of options for creating hip lines. By blending minor and major pentatonic shapes over a parallel root (e.g., G minor pentatonic and G major pentatonic over G7) and filling in the blanks with Mixolydian scale tones (e.g., G Mixolydian over G7), you have an almost fail-safe recipe for creating killer country lines. Factor in some chromatic embellishments, and you'll be ready to saddle up!

This first country example includes two separate phrases—motifs A (ascending) and B (descending). Both motifs occur in the open position and fit snugly within a garden-variety open G chord. When practicing this, try to let the notes bleed together as much as possible.

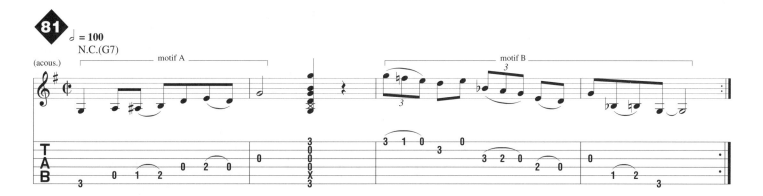

This next lick incorporates a healthy dose of chromaticism, hammer-ons, and pull-offs into a four-bar phrase, again spawned from an open-position G chord. Though the accompanying audio depicts this lick played on an electric, attack it from an acoustic angle as well.

Once you get a handle on these types of licks, in addition to practicing them pickstyle, try playing them using *hybrid picking* (i.e., "pick-and-fingers technique"). With a little woodshedding, you may find that this approach provides you with more versatility; the combination of pick and fingers makes it possible to painlessly alternate between Travis picking patterns and burning, pickstyle single-note lines without dropping a beat (or the pick!).

Another right-hand approach worth pursuing is referred to as claw picking. This technique involves plucking the strings in fingerstyle fashion, alternating between your thumb and index fingers exclusively. Insofar as this approach relates to conventional pickstyle technique, in *claw picking*, the thumb is used in place of a downstroke, while the index finger takes the place of a picked upstroke. In the end, this "clawing" right-hand approach produces all sorts of unpredictable accents, created in particular by the index finger, as it's used to pull on a string and then release it against the fretboard to create various snaps and pops.

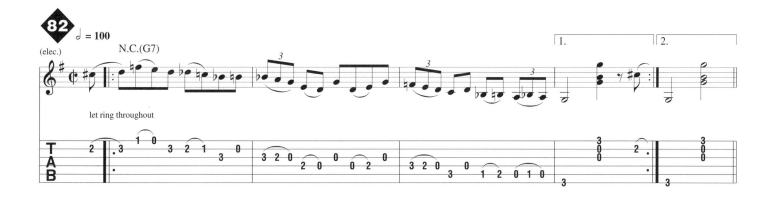

DOUBLE STOPS

Double stops are also par for the course in country music, and sound equally at home on both acoustic and electric instruments. These types of licks involve the performance of accented note pairs—interval shapes like thirds, sixths, and the occasional tritone—amidst intermittent single-note phrases. In most cases, double stops are performed using the aforementioned pick-and-fingers or claw-picking techniques, allowing the fingers to pull on the strings, creating rhythmic snaps and pops. In the following figure, try plucking every double stop with the middle and ring fingers of your picking hand, and use the pick to play each single note that occurs. Once you get this one down, try transposing the lick to other key areas.

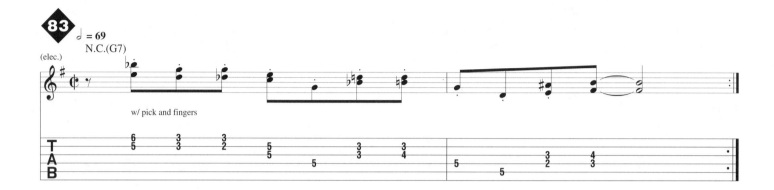

In the hands of a virtuoso, double stops can be used to push a solo over the top, as their extra density—two-notes picked or plucked simultaneously—automatically creates more intensity.

This next lick is performed over a C7 chord and uses plenty of major and minor thirds moved diatonically along the neck within the C Mixolydian mode (C–D–E–F–G–A–Bb). These thirds are also often embellished with chromatic passing tones, with most of the chromatic activity confined to the lower string of each note pair. Notice that these double stops, which occur exclusively on string set 1-2 or 2-3, are frequently alternated with single notes confined to the fourth string. This approach is exploited in the first measure of the following figure. When practicing the first measure, try viewing each individual single note that occurs along the fourth string collectively with the double stop that precedes it, regarding the combined unit as a triad. This will provide you with a greater understanding of how these types of licks are constructed. Then experiment with moving diatonic triads along the fretboard, practicing them in a similar manner, and try to come up with your own variations. Again, try plucking the double stops using your middle and ring fingers, then use your pick to play each single note that comes along.

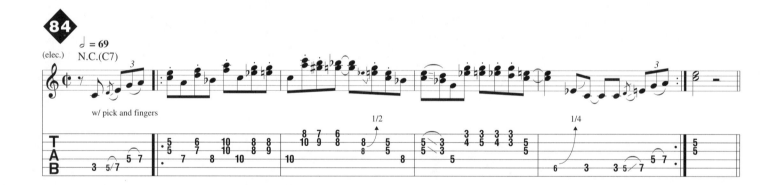

Double stops can also be used in conjunction with fret-hand pitch bends. These types of licks are most effective on an electric guitar with a light string gauge.

In the following lick, you can see that by simply bending the lower note of various double stops up the appropriate interval to reach the next higher diatonic pitch, some killer country licks can be created. These same notes can also be "prebent"—bending a note before striking it—and released to achieve a "backwards bend" effect, as in measure 4. Make sure that you practice these types of licks on a guitar with a fixed bridge (i.e., nontremolo); otherwise, your bending action will force all the neighboring strings to go flat, creating ghastly intonation problems.

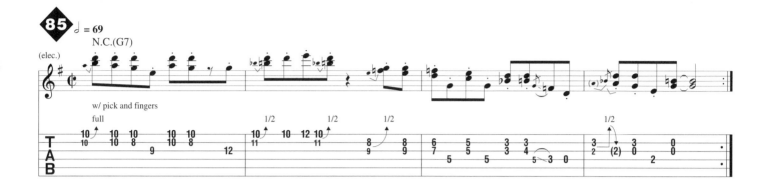

SINGLE-NOTE LICKS COMBINED WTIH BENDS

Another classic country soloing approach—particularly for electric guitarists—involves using "held bends" in conjunction with single-note lines. Similar to the prebend encountered in the previous example, held bends involve striking a lower string, bending it to a particular pitch, and holding that bend while higher strings are sounded. In the two licks that follow, this concept is explored in a descending format, suitable for performance over G7 and C7, respectively.

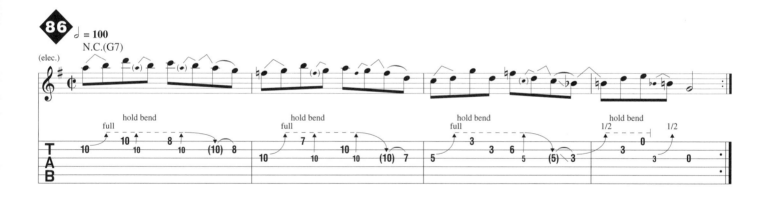

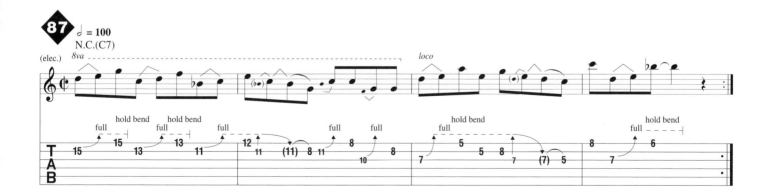

PEDAL-STEEL LICKS

If you're playing a country tune on an electric guitar and get the opportunity to accompany a vocalist or another soloist, one of the coolest things to do is cop a few licks that emulate a pedal steel. By combining bends with stationary notes in a manner similar to the previous examples, playing with the appropriate clean tone, and manipulating your guitar's volume control (or using a volume pedal), you can create the illusion of a whole other instrument!

The following figure is an example of playing changes using a pedal-steel approach. Note the emphasis on chord tones in each passing bar. By bending the second or third strings into notes that outline a dominant seventh chord (e.g., A7, D7, E7), not only does the phrase pack enough harmonic punch to outline the chord changes, a semblance of a melodic line is created.

Because these types of licks involve a gradual volume swell into the intended note, you may need to spend a few minutes practicing your timing. Since this example features two bends per bar, intended to sound squarely on beats 1 and 3, you'll need to strike the strings—with your guitar's volume shut off—a millisecond before each bending phrase begins, then gradually turn up your guitar's volume to swell the envelope of sound. With a little elbow grease, you'll be able to control these types of volume-manipulated licks so they peak at the precise rhythmic moment you're shooting for.

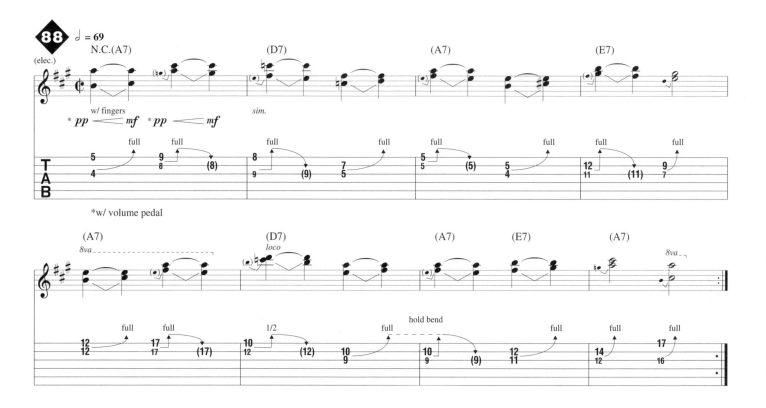

42

BANJO LICKS

The figure below is a classic bluegrass-inspired banjo riff. Presented here in the key of G, this passage can easily be transposed to fit any key by using a capo (refer to p. 47). Played pickstyle throughout, these types of figures make great intros into a barn-burning bluegrass number. For best results, try experimenting with your electric guitar's timbre, using either the bridge or middle pickup (w/ clean tone) and picking near the bridge to cop the nasal "plink" associated with a banjo.

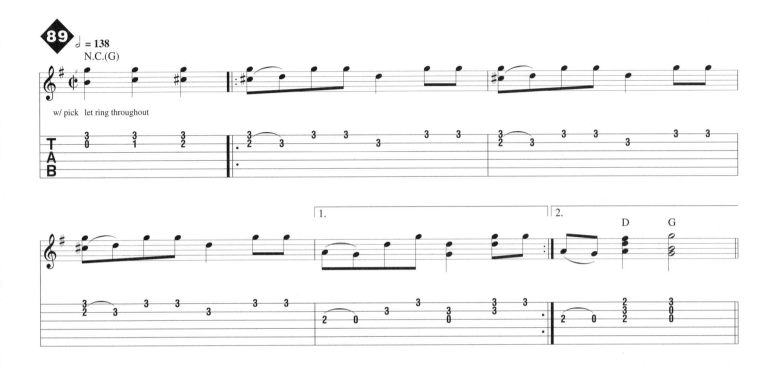

Banjo rolls can also be adapted to electric guitar. By using a combination of open strings and hammer-ons/pull-offs, in conjunction with fretted shapes outlining dominant seventh chords, you'll have burning arpeggio licks to whip out in the middle of a country solo. Because these types of figures imply harmony, licks like these can also be performed unaccompanied. Imagine the reaction you'll get if you unleash this type of lick while your band lays out a few bars for a "stop time" guitar break!

JAZZ

ARPEGGIOS AND OCTAVE SHAPES

In jazz, because the chords you're soloing over usually occur in ii–V–I cycles, you'll need to develop lines that outline these types of progressions and be comfortable using them in several keys if you want to "nail the changes." This can be done by superimposing *arpeggios*—playing the actual notes used to form each chord—over any given harmonic structure.

Factor octave shapes into the arpeggio equation, articulating them using your pick hand's thumb to warm up each note's attack *á la* Wes Montgomery, and you'll sound like an authentic "old school" jazzer. The following lick is performed using thumbed octaves exclusively, and outlines a ii–V–I–vi progression in C, jazzed up with the occasional chromatic passing tone and altered note.

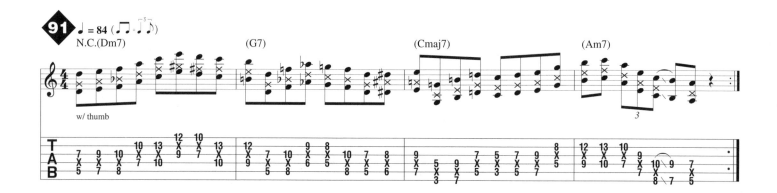

MELODIC MINOR, DIMINISHED, AND MAJOR PENTATONIC SCALES

This next lick focuses on different types of scales commonly employed when playing over jazz changes. The phrase begins with motif A—a descending Dm9(maj7) lick in measure 1, borrowed from the D melodic minor scale (D–E–F–G–A–B–C#). After picking the ninth—E—with a downstroke, use a singular upstroke to articulate the ensuing Dm triad (D–F–A). In the second measure (motif B), the diminished scale (G–Ab–A#–B–C#–D–E–F) is employed over G7, touching upon hip altered tones like b9 (Ab), #9 (A#), and #11 (C#). Over the Cmaj7 chord in measure 3 (motif C), C major pentatonic (C–D–E–G–A) is broken up into fourths and other interesting intervals, adding a somewhat jagged edge to the overall line. Finally, motif D in measure 4 depicts a descending flurry of notes straight out of an Am9 arpeggio (A–C–E–G–B).

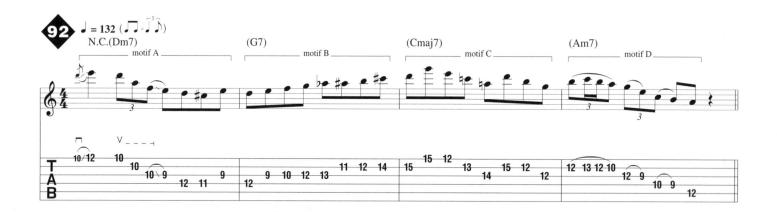

TRIPLETS, SWEEP PICKING, AUGMENTED TRIADS, AND THE WHOLE-TONE SCALE

Triplets also can be used to impart a jazz flavor to your lines. This rhythmic subdivision was a mainstay throughout jazz's bebop era and, if you find yourself playing over tunes written by Charlie Parker, Dizzy Gillespie, or Thelonious Monk, will likely raise the eyebrows of fellow bandmembers.

The following lick uses the triplet rhythm almost exclusively and involves a permutation of the same fretboard shape to accommodate each passing chord. In measure 1 (motif A), a Dm7 chord (D–F–A–C) is arpeggiated verbatim, presented in a pattern that combines pull-offs and sweep picking. By the second bar, this pattern morphs to outline a pair of augmented triad shapes—C# (C#–F–A) and A+ (A–C#–F). This phrase (motif B) is spiced up further by incorporating the whole-tone scale (G–A–B–C#–D#–F) to access the #11/♭5 and #5/♭13. C Lydian (C–D–E–F#–G–A–B) is employed over the Cmaj7 chord in measure 3, jazzed up with a little chromaticism along the second string. The phrase ends with a descending Am7 arpeggio (A–C–E–G) shape, featuring chromatic movement between the C and A along the fourth string.

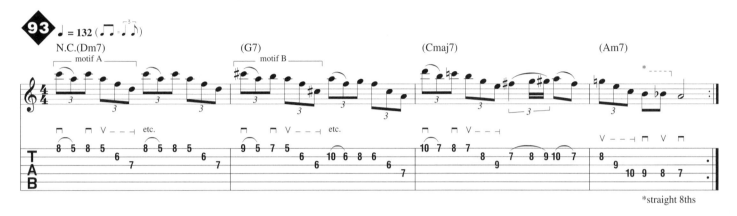

TRITONE SUBSTITUTION

As we discovered back in the jazz accompaniment patterns section, triads a tritone away from the root of a dominant seventh chord can be used to access hip altered tones. This same approach can be applied to your single-note lines as a means of generating "outside"-sounding licks. By arpeggiating a D♭ triad (D♭–F–A♭) over G7, the #11 (C#/D♭) and ♭9 (A♭) will automatically work their way into your lines.

The following example depicts a ii°–V–i in C minor. After a stream of chromaticism is employed over the Dm7♭5 chord, a D♭ triad (highlighted) is arpeggiated over G7 in the second bar. For the final phrase beginning in measure 3, the C Dorian scale (C–D–E♭–F–A–B♭) is used, but ventures into outside territory in the last measure when a major triad—G♭ (G♭–B♭–D♭)—is superimposed a tritone away from the root. This is a hip way to sound "out" over a tonic minor chord.

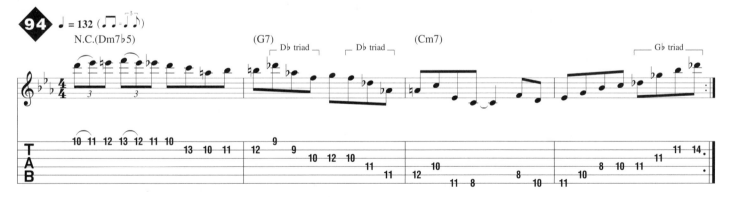

ROCK

MULTIPURPOSE LICKS

Whether you play hard rock, classic rock, southern rock, '70s metal, or grunge, nothing sounds more appropriate at the peak of a guitar solo than "looping" (i.e., repeating) minor pentatonic licks. These types of pentatonic patterns usually involve working between no more than a couple of strings, rapidly repeating the same note sequence—typically between two and six notes. In some circles, these are referred to as "smear licks"—particularly when they're played as fast as possible, with no regard for the song's tempo, floating over the pulse of the music in manic fashion.

The several figures that follow depict classic "smear" licks, most of which are centered at the twelfth fret in E minor pentatonic (E–G–A–B–D). Breaking into these types of patterns at the high point of a solo will get the crowd on their feet.

TRANSPOSITION
MOVABLE FORMS, CAPOS, AND OTHER MUSICIANS' TRICKS

Once you're physically able to play the riffs and licks covered in the previous chapters, the next step is to "own" them—to be able to transpose or permutate them on the fly. In short, the more music theory training and chord/scale/arpeggio study on the guitar fretboard you have, the more successful you'll be at implementing your vast vocabulary of riffs and licks. But don't fret if you feel your theory chops aren't up to this task: The vast majority of guitarists responsible for defining the instrument's role in blues, country, and rock got by just fine without knowing much more than the names of the chords they were playing!

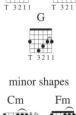

TAKING ADVANTAGE OF MOVABLE FORMS

If you don't have the ability to transpose your riffs and licks, you'll be stuck playing the same phrases in the same songs until you're old and gray. But you'd be surprised how a simple study in "fretboard geography" can give your "pet phrases" more mileage. If you learn your riffs and licks in relation to basic barre chords shapes, when it comes time to unload your vocabulary in a different key, you'll be more than halfway there.

Try this approach using some of the "Hendrix-style" accompaniment patterns on page 29. First, take the opening C chord shape that houses the initial "Hendrix" phrase, and move it along the fretboard to create F (root on first fret, sixth string) and G (root on third fret, sixth string). Next, practice moving this shape "in time" to the aforementioned fretting positions so it implies a four-bar C–F–C–G progression. The final step is to incorporate variations of the Hendrix-type rhythm fills into these shifting shapes. As an exercise, try strumming each chord for two beats, then cram in the appropriate major pentatonic-based fill so it fits over beats 3 and 4. Now take the same approach with your minor barre chord shapes and minor pentatonic fills, plugging them into a four-bar Cm–Fm–Cm–Gm progression. Then try to mix up major and minor shapes in an Em–D–C–G progression, or something even more involved—like C–G–Am–Em–F–C–F–G.

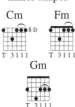

In short, if you come to rely on this transposing approach, this heightened awareness of available chord shapes will provide you with a host of options. With time and practice, you'll be able to grab the appropriate—and most convenient—chord anywhere on the neck, making it possible to tap into other options in your musical vocabulary, instead of moving the exact same lick along the fretboard and restating it verbatim.

USING A CAPO

Let's say that you learned a bunch of tunes for an upcoming country gig. The songs on the reference recording you were given were originally all performed in "guitar-friendly" keys like C, G, D, A, and E. Since that's a walk in the park for us guitar players, you know this gig's going to be easy money. But when you get to the club that night, your band's singer is nowhere to be found. It turns out, he's sent a sub—a female vocalist. And this woman is not your average yodeler either—she's the best country singer in your town. Being that she's a top-notch professional, she already knows every tune in the book, so rehearsal isn't necessary—heck, you go on in fifteen minutes anyway! However, in strong contrast to the vocal veteran, your band doesn't perform by the "book"—the only country tunes you all know together are the ones you prepared for this evening's set. What's wrong with this picture? Because the female voice typically sits in a higher register than the male's (and it's obviously too late to learn new tunes), you're going to have to adapt every song you've learned to her vocal range. It's moments like this when you pray you left your capo in your guitar's case!

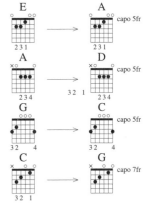

When it comes time to transpose a tune that revolves exclusively around open-position "cowboy" chords, a capo can be a lifesaver. In the above-described scenario, your vocalist would likely know what key she prefers to sing each particular tune in. If she calls the key of A for a song that you learned in E, you'll need to employ the capo as a "new nut." In this case, since the original key's tonic chord (E) has its low root located on the open sixth string, all you need to do is find the root of the new key's tonic chord (A) on that same string and strap a capo across the appropriate fret (V). Similarly, a shift from the key of A (root on open fifth string) to D (root moved to fifth fret of fifth string) could be achieved by placing a capo across the fifth fret. Transposing to keys where the tonic chord's root is fretted (e.g., G or C) is a little more tricky, but it's still the same principle: targeting the open strings. To transpose open-position chords from the key of G to C, first observe the open strings inherent to your G chord. Next, find the same open-string interval layout (analyze which chord tones are the root, third, and fifth, for instance) on a higher fret that corresponds to the pitches from a C triad (C–E–G). You'll find the only location housing this same grouping of open-string pitches is across the fifth fret. Similarly, a transposition from open-position C to G could be achieved by slapping a capo across the seventh fret.

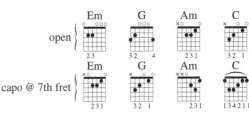

To really get comfortable with a capo, try taking a basic open-position based progression—like Em–G–Am–C—and play the identical progression (in the same key) at different capoed locations. (Note: you'll also need to use an occasional barre chord.) The first step is to convert your starting chord to a different "physical" open-position shape (e.g., Am or Dm). Try placing your capo across the seventh fret—where the open fifth string under the "new nut" would be an E—then play a garden-variety Am chord shape. This shape superimposed over the seventh fret will create the sound of an Em chord. Similarly, the user-friendly open-position C shape would sound as a G chord when played with the seventh fret capoed. Meanwhile, Am could be created by superimposing the basic Dm shape at that new capoed spot. Since none of the "new" open strings across the seventh fret are chord tones from C, you'll have to resort to using a barre chord. For this, just plug in your basic "F" barre chord shape across the eighth fret. For a little adventure, try working out the same sounding progression (i.e., not transposed) with the capo positioned across the fifth and tenth frets.

JAZZ AND STUDIO MUSICIAN LINGO

In certain circles, there are shorthand methods for indicating what key a song is to be played in. If you're unfamiliar with these types of gestures, you may be in for a rude awakening the next time you sub for the guitar player in your friend's jazz band. For example: What does it mean if the leader of your jazz combo, shortly before counting off a tune, sticks out his arm and points three fingers straight down to the ground? Answer: "Three fingers down" means that tune, regardless of what key you originally learned it in, is going to be performed in a key with three flats ("♭") that night, meaning either E♭ major or C minor (the relative minor). Similarly, "three fingers up" means the song will be transposed to a key with three sharps ("♯"), meaning either A major or F♯ minor. Imagine how horrible that tune's gonna sound if everybody in the band sees your leader's hand signal but you! You'll be playing in the wrong key, wishing you packed some razor blades in your guitar case! Even worse, if you don't know your key signatures in the first place, you're going to wish you never answered your buddy's phone call! Again, another incentive to become "musically literate."

Studio musicians also have to adapt to certain shorthand methods for indicating a song's key and progression. In Nashville, for instance, a chord chart distributed at a session typically consists of numbers (e.g., 1–4–5) as opposed to traditional chord symbols (e.g., B♭–E♭–F). The contractor or producer of that recording date will simply tell you what key the song section will be performed in, and you're expected to use your awareness of diatonic harmony and plug in the appropriate chords that correspond to the numbers appearing on the chart. Once again, music theory knowledge can make or break your ability to "survive"— in this case, while the tape is rolling and the clock is ticking in a pricey studio! Hmmm. Could a pattern be emerging here?

NASHVILLE CHART

Key of C 4/4				V–II			
				1	1	4	1
				5	4	1	2/5
Intro: Guitar Only				1	4	1	1
5	4	1	1	4	5	1	1
5	4	1	1				
				C–II			
Band in– Verse 1				4	5	1	1
1	1	4	1	2	2	3	3
5	4	1	2/5	4	5	1	1
1	4	1	1	5	5	1	1
4	5	1	1	4	5	1	①
				◇	END		
Chorus I							
4	5	1	1				
2	2	5	5				
4	5	1	1				
5	5	◇	1				
Solo							
4	4	4/5	1				
6⁻	4	5	⑤◇				

2/5	Two beats of 2-chord, then two beats of 5-chord.
⑤◇	Whole note on 5-chord.
①	This chord is held two beats instead of four.
6⁻	6-chord is a Minor 7th.

NASHVILLE SYSTEM

Key	♯'s / ♭'s	1	2	3	4	5	6	7
C		C	Dm	Em	F	G	Am	B°
C♯/D♭	♯♯♯♯♯♯♯ / ♭♭♭♭♭	C♯/D♭	D♯m/E♭m	E♯m/Fm	F♯/G♭	G♯/A♭	A♯m/B♭m	B♯°/C°
D	♯♯	D	Em	F♯m	G	A	Bm	C♯°
E♭	♭♭♭	E♭	Fm	Gm	A♭	B♭	Cm	D°
E	♯♯♯♯	E	F♯m	G♯m	A	B	C♯m	D♯°
F	♭	F	Gm	Am	B♭	C	D♯m	E°
F♯/G♭	♯♯♯♯♯♯ / ♭♭♭♭♭♭	F♯/G♭	G♯m/A♭m	A♯m/B♭m	B/C♭	C♯/D♭	D×m/E♭m	E×m/F°
G	♯	G	Am	Bm	C	D	Em	F♯°
A♭	♭♭♭♭	A♭	B♭m	Cm	Db	Eb	Fm	G°
A	♯♯♯	A	Bm	C♯m	D	E	F♯m	G♯°
B♭	♭♭	Bb	Cm	Dm	Eb	F	Gm	A°
B	♯♯♯♯♯	B	C♯m	D♯m	E	F♯	G♯m	A♯°